Evil and Silence

Evil

and

Silence

Richard Fleming

Paradigm Publishers
Boulder • London

Copyright © 2010 Paradigm Publishers

Published in the United States by Paradigm Publishers, 2845 Wilderness Place, Suite 200, Boulder, CO 80301 USA.

Paradigm Publishers is the trade name of Birkenkamp & Company, LLC, Dean Birkenkamp, President and Publisher.

Library of Congress Cataloging-in-Publication Data

Fleming, Richard, 1952–
  Evil and silence / Richard Fleming.
      p. cm.
  Includes index.
  ISBN 978-1-59451-728-0 (hardcover : alk. paper)
  ISBN 978-1-59451-729-7 (paperback : alk. paper)
  1. Good and evil. 2. Nonviolence. 3. Silence. 4. Violence. 5. Oral communication. 6. Conduct of life. I. Title.
  BJ1401.F56 2009
  170—dc22

                                                              2009011945

Printed and bound in the United States of America on acid-free paper that meets the standards of the American National Standard for Permanence of Paper for Printed Library Materials.

Designed and Typeset by Straight Creek Bookmakers.
13 12 11   2 3 4 5

Foreword

The care that we must take with each word we speak and each step we take can hardly be overstated. It is commonplace for us to say "that is not what I meant" or "I did not intend for that to happen." We frequently find ourselves insisting "you did not hear me correctly" or "I would not have done that if I had known this would be the case"; or asserting "I wish I had never said or done those things" or "I meant something else entirely." We often want our words and deeds back. The inevitable loss of control over meaning what we say, over how others understand us and how our words are used, and the constant failure of safely knowing what will truly result from what we do, produce, for many of us, quiet desperation. Similarly, when confronted with the torment and evil of our existence, we often can do no more than shake our heads, saying nothing, finding no words, "having literally nothing to say." On these occasions, we naturally have no meaningful words, although we repeatedly turn from that critical condition to one of speaking, to saying something or just anything. Accordingly, this text seeks to provide an attentiveness of such weight to talk and action that the question of whether to

v

say or do anything at all is consequential. ["How to improve the world (you will only make matters worse)."]

The reader should not be surprised, therefore, that it is a *relentless reflection* on the shared words we commonly use and inhabit that controls (directs and restrains) the discussions in the following pages. This is an effort to determine and express, in the achievements of traditional and recent philosophy, justifiable rules of action for our existence and subsistence, as well as to offer and agree on descriptions yet unsaid of the ordinary, of the conditions that make possible what we say and do. As a result, one aim of this book is to establish some of the first words and steps required in clearly contemplating evil and violence and in understanding the meaningful place of good and nonviolence in our talk and silence.

This book can be read productively, I believe, by any appropriately curious and reflective individual. Such an open but rational and disciplined temperament, whether it is natural or induced, serves one well, I would think, to find some good in what follows. There are introductory remarks at the beginnings of both the First and Second Books (1–8, 61–65) to help establish context for the reader; and constant repetition of material—given throughout the individual sections and exertions of thought—should assist the reader further. Therefore, other than being brought up in sound habits and possessing right dispositions, anyone approaching and contemplating the ensuing paragraphs and ancillary presentations should have only normal difficulties in working with the philosophical ideas pursued. The general form of the text of separate remarks in separate books with supplementary materials primarily follows Schopenhauer's *The World as Will and Representation*. That is the main textual mold into which the various words, texts, and authors are poured. Additionally, even though the supplementary material is intended to be just that—supplementary to the First Book and Second Book—the reader may wish to investigate these pages ahead of a full reading of the rest of the text, as many issues about writing, reading, arguments, and sources are directly discussed there, including references to many musical works that are integral to the text. For links to the musical references mentioned in the supplements, please go to the Web page for this book:

www.paradigmpublishers.com/books/BookDetail
.aspx?productID=215102

Of course, the reasons for such form and content presentation are connected with the very nature of the investigation of *Evil and Silence,* which a reader will recognize as they read more and more of a text of "words not my own." However, even with all that being said, it is still likely that the text will be understood best by someone who has already said or read many of the words that are used in it—or at least similar words. So it is not a moral handbook or philosophical primer, although its material has defined courses of my teaching. Its purpose would be achieved if it gave pause to a person or two who reread its words and listened to them in a renewed way. I should not like my writing to spare others the trouble of listening and thinking but rather, if possible, to awaken for them sounds and thoughts not their own.

[This text is probably best read as a continuation of *First Word Philosophy* (2004). Rather than identifying and articulating the basic principles and methods of ordinary language philosophy—one of whose central subjects is the justice of speech and which has as a central concern the task of accepting finitude, returning words to their everyday use—these pages are a concentrated application of those fundamentals. Each numbered remark is a separate exercise of thought governed by a variety of people's words but usually with a particular voice dominating. My linking or writing of the sections produces the general movement of the text. It begins, after an introductory discussion, with Socrates and ends with Cage. To that extent, the preferred title of this current work would simply be *Philosophical Exercises: Socrates to Cage.*]

If these pages have any value, it rests in the fact that arguments are expressed in them (this is not the place for indignation or aphoristic wisdom), and in this regard the clearer the arguments the greater will be the value. Recognition of the fact of evil (First Book) and the ways of making a life worth living in the face of that fact (Second Book) are points of contention and lines of reasoning inhabiting the connecting exercises of the text. There is no "answering" evil, and the first efforts of consequence beyond that acknowledgment are listening attentively to the silence that surrounds us, affirming the limits of sound, and creating rather than negating with our talk and actions. These statements (and others) are to be made perspicuous and convincing in the arguments to follow. Here I am conscious of having fallen a long way short of what is possible and needed, but it seems preferable to make this effort as opposed to showing how obscure everything is—there may be time to go into that (although there is seemingly no lack of such presentation) when we are within measurable distance of achieving logical clarity on the matters at hand.

—RF
NYC, Winter 2009

Contents

First Book

Just Plain Evil

I am tempted to tell you that it so happens that we are fighting ... fighting for justifiable distinctions. The kind of distinctions that are as important as humans themselves ... between sacrifice and ideology, between cogency and violence, between strength and cruelty, for that even more vital distinction between the sensible and the nonsensible.

Contents

Preliminary Remark

This First Book shows, I trust, the importance of accepting the fact of evil and demonstrates the logic of nonviolence and the lack thereof of violence. Its sense might be summed up in the following words: Neither to do wrong nor to return a wrong is ever right. This is certainly not an original proposition or a unique conclusion, but I do not wish to judge how far my efforts coincide with those of other philosophers. Indeed, what I have written here makes no claim to novelty in general or in detail. (In fact, it loudly proclaims to be only the words of others—it is best to avoid the beginnings of evil.*) I will only mention that beyond the ordinary language philosophers, I am indebted to Dostoevsky's great works and to the writings of Camus and the lucid thought and life of Socrates for much of the stimulation of the arguments and many of the reflections of these pages.

[*The reader will have been already overwhelmed by this fact—whether it is the *Tractatus* material in the foreword or that from "Letters to a German Friend" on the previous page.]

We talk and act.

1. The world is our word. It wears the colors and expresses the sounds it does by means of the things we say and do. A word has meaning in its use, in the context of a sentence. A sentence has meaning in a language and a language requires a form of life. A form of life has significance only in a world. A world has meaning within the context of a word. There is more to the world, to be sure, than we can talk about, more than we can say about any particular world or aspect of the world ["I can't put it in words, you must experience it for yourself," "what we continue to face and live with is not to be described or explained," "that world is strange and incomprehensible to me"]; but it is empty to suggest the world might be different from what we do or say, as there is no possibility of our having any demonstration or representation of how it might be different from any way in which we might talk about or act in it. "Different from what?" would be the pressing

question posed in such a context or elicited by such a claim. It might be objected that facts simply are and we humans try our best to come to terms with them. But this, of course, had to be said, and no matter how hard we try to imagine a world of mere fact, without even the word "fact" with which to think and speak of it, the moment we try to give shape to these inchoate imaginings we must use words. It is seductive to consider a fact-in-itself, but a fact "as such" would be something we could literally say nothing about, must necessarily be silent about. The world may be independent of my will, but the issue is what language relates the world to be. We can say that the world faces us as a brute fact. It does not speak to our sufferings and longings. It does not answer our anguished cries for understanding. It tells us nothing. It is audible and inarticulate. And still the world is our word. The limits of our language mean the limits of our world.

2. Talk and action are materially inseparable. This is the fact of language. Our acting and speaking together is an announcement that the fact of language is more telling than any fact uttered within it, that every fact that a disciplined life asserts utters the fact of language. Talking, whether asking questions, giving directions, or reporting events, is doing something and acting in some particular way. Without the actions that accompany our asking, telling, or reporting, significant linguistic expression could not be. To imagine a language is to imagine a form of life. Similarly, acting, whether running, crying, or shopping, is possible only because there is talk or language in which we can distinguish one action from another. Human action does not identify itself or tell us how it is to be clearly differentiated and recognized. It is by means of talk that actions are established and demarcated. Running and crying and shopping are different activities because there are rules of language that distinguish them and give them their identity. There is no Archimedean point from which talk and action can be unraveled. We seek to perceive them, and we do not see them; we seek to hear them, and we do not hear them; identified within the overlapping, crisscrossing fibers of all things, they cannot be separated from each other without losing them. So even though we might isolate or simplify, for a particular purpose, certain language uses or certain human actions, this effort

and distinction is but an intellectual abstraction or a product of ideological or pedagogical thinking, and it must not make us forget the factual inseparability of talk and action.

3. Language and world exist in harmony. We could not do and say the things we do if this was not the case, if there was not a concordance of world and word. (It is agreement not of choice but of fact, i.e., the objectivity of language and existence.) Such unity allows us to do what we do. To say falsely "this is red" requires that humans and the world be of a like nature and be in agreement with each other. Otherwise we could not so talk. We could not speak truthfully or falsely, recognize sameness or difference, fail to say what we mean, or find our pain inexpressible without an agreement and harmony of humans and the world. Thus we come to see, at this level of investigation, this registrar of reflection, that the idea of agreement with reality does not have any clear application, because its use presupposes the agreement. When we examine what we should say when, what words we should use in what situations, we are looking again not *merely* at words (or "meanings," whatever they may be) but also at the realities we use the words to talk about: We are using a sharpened awareness of words to sharpen our perception of, though not as the final arbiter of, the phenomena. To solve our philosophical problems, to recognize the important facts of philosophical investigations, we must place the words and meanings of philosophical interest in alignment with their ordinary controls and observe the natural unity of the factual and the conceptual.

4. There is an unfated connection between meaning and saying. A constant struggle with how others can and do understand us and us them is part of the task of our ordinary lives. (The composition of finitude is fundamental to the philosophical exercises in which we now find ourselves.) The continual possibility of failing to mean what we say is always before us. A loss of control of our words, which is an inevitable part of talk because our words leave us on their saying, threatens madness and a loss of ourselves. Our loss of control is not necessarily over what words mean (we can fully know what words can mean, what they can be used to say or imply) but over what we mean in using them when and where we do. We do not command the context of language

use in which we speak. We have a (or some) choice over our words but not the same authority over their meanings. Living a life (a philosophical or tolerantly reflective life) that recognizes the unfated connection of meaning and saying can be to live a life of quiet desperation. Not knowing how to mean or say what we wish naturally numbs us, reintroduces silence, and places the necessity of beginning again before us. However, remembering the fact and uses of language that make such a life possible can offer understanding and perspective. It offers, for instance, a way to resist claims such as "all is permitted" and "only I know if I am in pain" and efforts that allow crime to set the law, murderers to be judges, and violence to establish morality.

5. The ordinary is unapproachable. It is everywhere we are. There is no getting closer to it, no approach, because we *are* as close as possible. Our philosophy and task take the form of becoming more reflectively aware of what we already know, of the ordinary. We know (at this level of our reflection) how to talk and use language, so we can expect few new or esoteric discoveries about our ways of speaking, but we may find instead only reminders of what we cannot not know. ["I did not notice or suspect many things that lay under my nose; I did not guess at the kindliness in the midst of the enmity."] What we must do is look more carefully at the familiar, at that of which we take no notice because it is always with us. The ordinary is not that taken as a *given* (as though it were a hypothesis) but is that taken for *granted*. It is our shared, common existence that is in plain view, the conditions of possibility of word and world. The fact that we learn language and master its use makes possible the things we say and do. (How do I know that this is red? I have *learned* English.) It is, of course, to be noticed that talk of the everyday and the ordinary is sometimes rather prevalent, as many conversations and disciplines seem to find such an appeal helpful in one way or another and at one time or another. However, seldom are these discussions relevant to or cognizant of the philosophical temperament that guides us here, for such talk and presentation are almost always providing ways to approach the ordinary. They are giving analysis rather than investigating the conditions that make analysis possible, rather than speaking of the ways we live

our skepticism. It is true that the ordinary can become an object of inquiry or investigation. Even the ordinary can be extraordinary. But it is then not the ordinary as here described, for it (the ordinary) remains that which makes possible the investigation of the "ordinary." We must not fall into equivocation. Talk of returning to, or finding again, or unveiling the ordinary does not make it or show it approachable, show it to be an object for analysis and discovery, but reminds us that we can talk of it and puzzle over it like any other concept. In so doing we must remember what makes such talk possible and what we are trying to do. This "talk of the ordinary" will not get us nearer or between or provide needed unity to our talk and action, language and world. We are already as close as we can be to the ordinary. There is no explanation of it, no advancement toward it, that can be given or taken properly; only further descriptions of it can be offered.

6. There is a logic to each word we speak. Our philosophy describes the ordinary and investigates the constraints and entanglements of language use not by rhetoric, or by any of the arts of persuasion, but by the clarity of unswerving reason and self-reflection. It is a work of logic. There is a systematic order to each context of language use, and only by attention to that order, to what we should and do say when, is an illusory clarity of inquiry avoided. That is the reason for sometimes saying "a" logic rather than just "logic." The latter use is preferable but may not emphasize strongly enough the particularity of what we are investigating or asking—certainly there is no intended conflict of understanding between the two uses here. The context dependence of our logical investigations is emphasized in claims like: "'What is reality?' is a question that can only give rise to nonsense." "What we ordinarily say and mean may have a direct and deep control over what we philosophically say and mean." "Our problems are not abstract but perhaps the most concrete that there are." Here at last we should be able to dissolve many of our problems, release difficulties, and move forward on agreeing about how to reach agreement. Such an essential concern was seen and claimed by Socrates when he first betook himself to the way of words; and it was pursued in the metaphysical and ethical writings of Aristotle and, later, by Camus and Austin in such subjects as

"the justice of speech." One moral of a philosophy with an attention to ordinary use is that it is *in* the threaded linguistic data and the conditions that make possible that data, in the logic of every word we speak, that we can (at least in part) find ourselves. That is where we are. It is an effort to understand not me but *us*, what *we* do; to understand *our* philosophy, as Wittgenstein calls it. Investigating and learning the logic of words not my own means *waiting* on the words of others. Our philosophy often thereby invites silence. But when conceit or tricks of language contribute to maintaining an abuse or a suffering that can be addressed or possibly relieved, then to speak out in return and show the obscenity hidden under the verbal cloak might be worth an effort of logical responsiveness.

7. A respect for the ordinary is a necessary beginning. From a description of the ordinary and the fact of language we pursue an understanding of what choices of action can and cannot be logically justified. But can we deduce, logically, a rule of behavior (justified action) from awareness of the fact that we talk and act? Whatever values and rules are found they are not "given from on high" but must be inferred from the conditions of living and be consistent with the limits of the possible ways we can meaningfully talk and act. Whereas a traditional philosopher often tries to fill the "discovered gap" between thoughts and actions, the inner and outer, between feelings and arguments, with god or universals, in order to gain harmony between mind and world, or denies theoretically that the gap can be addressed or filled (an abstract skepticism), such options are not open to one who restricts herself or himself to finding answers in the natural forms of life (i.e., in terms of the ordinary). When skepticism and dualism threaten, an abstract or ideological appeal or response is resisted and found wanting by the ordinary language philosopher and is replaced with reminders of our biological and conventional ways of living. There is nothing else that holds or can provide our beginnings, as these reminders are of the very general facts of nature or of human life against the background of which our concepts and logic mean anything at all. But this means that these traditional philosophical problems of doubt and separation and the various companion concerns should completely

disappear. They are solved not by giving new information but rather by rearranging and providing different ways to see what we have always known.

8. Living deliberately is the task of accepting finitude. The fact of language is that in terms of which all is and comes to be. In the midst of that fact, we find constraints and entanglements. We would like firm and complete assurances against these difficulties. We seek absolute foundations for the ways we think and act. Traditional epistemology and morality fail to provide these foundations. The attempt to satisfy the demand for the absolute makes what we say inherently private. It forces us to withhold our restricted, public, ordinary words not only from others but from ourselves. One of the intricacies of life and language that must be faced is that what we say or express may be meant or be used in a way we had not expected or wanted. The context of use in which we place our words is largely beyond our control. Thus the question of "whether we can mean (use) what we say" is often before us. Not all we say can be meant. The meaning of our words may be clear, but they still may not be meant, may not be capable of being used in this particular context on this particular occasion. Philosophical failures and disappointments force use back upon ourselves. An appreciation of the unfated connection between saying and meaning leads to varied and self-reflective senses and understandings of sentences like: "You should not have said that." "Do you know what you just said?" "Did you mean it?" "You can't say that! What do you mean?" "She cannot possibly have meant what she said." We can be critically questioned about what we say or do not say, but not as easily questioned for how what we say is used or comes to have a life of its own. Examination of ourselves reveals the threat of inexpressiveness and the need for others. (The language we learn was used before we were. Words are before I am.) Our attention to "what we cannot not know" instills a methodical, deliberate patience in our reflections, makes us less quick to judge what we hear others say and more careful about actually speaking what we can say. Our existence with others shows that we must accept the truth of these hesitations and live our skepticism. To do so, our philosophical reflections, descriptions, and arguments will impress on us a care that we

must take with each word we speak. It is a care that at times has what might be called an ethical force because it makes evident responsibilities of talk and consequential the question of whether to say anything at all.

Justifiable action is a question of harm.

9. Individual or collective action may not be just. What we say and do is not always warranted. Having gone therefore, at least temporarily, to the root of things (in our discussions of word, world, and the ordinary) it is important, existence being what it is, to know how to live and talk justly. Understanding the possible justifications for our actions and talk requires careful, quiet reflection on our conversations with others, including the conditions of possibility for such a life. (Accepting this need for conversation for a justifiable and moral life, yet suggesting the condition of "silence" as preparation for both the talk and its justification, does not seem an unhelpful proposal; but that is to get ahead of ourselves.) That is, once the conditions have been laid bare that make possible any distinctions of meaning and saying, once *the trust in common words* has been established, various philosophical exercises present themselves. Because a body (or possession of a body, like the claims of private ownership of anything) necessitates some violence, be it considered ever so little—in breathing and eating and walking, for instance—we might question how we can ever rightly or innocently act. Is it just to do good to our friends and harm to our enemies? Is it the part of a just person to injure any human being whatsoever? Such questions threaten to divide the self between efforts at justifications and revelations of who I am. Sometimes all we believe we can do with such questions is reply that our actions are based on no more reason than our revealed and unstudied desires. However, this often is held to be inadequate or too slight of a response, and we are expected to offer and dispute reasons that ground our actions, expected rationally to present arguments by way of answer. Revelations and justifications of self are often thereby placed at odds. But no such division should immediately bother us here because both efforts are linked by their common understanding of moral confrontation

as that of one person's examination of another. They are connected by the conversation that is required to assess my life and that is intended to make myself intelligible to others, by way of making myself intelligible to myself.

10. Justice, good, and virtue are mutually exclusive from harm, evil, and injustice. Empirical data and conceptual reflections support this claim. When would we say: a just injustice, a good evil, a harmful virtue, a harmful good, a just evil, an unjust virtue? What contexts of use would support such ways of speaking? Can we think of one? Or two? Just actions are not consistently undertaken, it would seem, to produce unjust results; virtue is not pursued to make people bad. Harm or injury are judged to be that which is bad and are generally opposite what is called and held to be good. Justice is good and injustice is bad. A just person does not seek to harm anyone, but the unjust does. It is impossible for just humans to seek meaningfully to make others unjust by justice or for good persons to try to make other persons bad by virtue. Injuring is not the work of the good but of its opposite. The just individual is good. To do wrong is never a virtue or good.

11. Injured or harmed humans are worse with respect to human virtue. To be injured is to be harmed or wounded or wronged. ["He was injured in the accident." "Her actions might have injured her chances." "I was injured by his words." "It was said in an injured tone." "She cannot do her work because she has been injured."] Sentences of "injured" use begin to provide the data for the reflections and argument that justice is a human virtue and human beings who are harmed necessarily become more unjust, that is, more removed from a life of quality and worth; so justice never is found in harm. Injury makes one less able to excel at what one does and less capable of justly acting and of being or trying to be just. It is apparent, then, that it is never just to injure anyone. Harm makes one worse or less excellent. When injured we are less able to do what it is of our best nature to do. Thus it is not the work of the just person to harm either a friend or anyone else, but of their opposite, the unjust person. No distinction between friend and enemy is useful here. It is never just to harm anyone, friend or enemy.

12. To do wrong or retaliate with a wrong is never right. Do we say that one must never in any way do wrong willingly, or must one do wrong in one way and not in another? One must never do wrong, for wrongdoing and injustice are in every way harmful and shameful to the perpetrator of wrong. Nor when wronged must one inflict wrong in return, as most believe, because one cannot justly do wrong. Mistreating people is no different from wrongdoing. One should never do wrong in return for a wrong, nor mistreat any human, no matter how one has been mistreated by another. Only a few people hold this view or will hold it, and there is the danger of losing or having no common ground for conversation between those who are guided by this thinking and those who are not, for they inevitably despise each other's views and will no longer listen to each other. ["The color you see before you is what *I* call blue." "The phenomenon described is what *I* call justice."] The basis of our deliberations, then, is that we agree and hold in common that neither to do wrong nor to return a wrong is ever right, nor is bad treatment in return for bad treatment ever justified. Do I say these things about the just and the wrong from my own experience? No, even if I have had such an experience. Conceptual reflection, objective argument, and logic support these contentions. However, if only because of the great potential for disagreement and animosity, we must not be too quick to push ahead to such and similar conclusions and to their implications. We must patiently reflect on such a basis of talk and express the logic of our agreement and philosophical understanding, even if death threatens, for it is much more difficult to avoid wickedness than death; wickedness runs faster than death.

13. Socratic questioning is a nonviolent activity that makes enemies. Socrates expresses claims and arguments many others will give, mangle, or vary, but not "in the embroidered and stylized phrases" used by so many others. Instead he does so in words spoken from the street, seemingly spontaneously, using the apparent first words that come to hand. It is a philosophy presented as being that of voice, not only of mind; a philosophy that recognizes that the justice of speech is its subject. As he says: I put my trust in the justice of what I say; it would not be fitting to toy with words. Here, in an admittedly ignorable

passage, though in an identifiable and useful sense, is philosophy tuned to the words we use, to the objectivity of language, to words at work, in application. It is an assertion of the reminders or demonstrated (necessary) consequences of our shared and common existence. It is agreeing about how to reach agreement. Whatever the subject matter, Socrates works to reach agreement and finds that effort of prime importance no matter how frustrating or tedious it becomes. Although seemingly innocuous, it is a dangerous philosophy. Consider: I tried to show him that he thought himself wise but that he was not. As a result he came to dislike me and so did many bystanders. It is a life that faces and cannot escape a constant foreboding. Of the many ways one may and must question the Platonic portrait of Socrates, one constant, nonignorable fact is that it is the state, and the life it proposes and enforces, that puts Socrates to death. It is an act whose intertwining of inevitability with a lack of necessity seems to establish the consequences of philosophy as such in the administrative, government world. A person who really fights for justice must lead, then, a restricted or dual life, not an open, civil life if he or she is to survive for even a short time. Such individuals may have to turn to living in silence.

14. One who does not know everything cannot justifiably destroy everything. Careful, reflective questioning of those who willingly harm others exposes an arrogance of wisdom, a refusal to accept limits to our (their) knowledge and actions. It is the denial of or indifference to these restrictions that often lead to deliberate choices of violence, injury, and hatred (definitive acts of feeling and bad argument). A thorough questioning of the propositions and principles of violence reveals efforts to mean what cannot be said when trying to justify retaliation, and talk of injustice as good, and harm as a virtue. The Socratic effort (and our public conversations) to uphold meaningful distinctions of justice and injustice, good and harm, true and false, and accept the consequences (the arguments and conclusions) of the distinctions must not go unexamined. (Austin was probably even more tenacious than Socrates in this regard. Just remember, for instance, his reminding us: "We don't, I think, claim to *know* by analogy, but only to *argue* by analogy" and "There is a singular difference

between the two forms of challenge: '*How* do you know?' and '*Why* do you believe?'" and "'It was a mistake,' 'It was an accident'—how readily these can *appear* indifferent, and even be used together.") If we make no effort to speak "the same language," to find objectivity in our language uses, to adhere to the consistency of the grammar of our lives, then violence and destruction are likely to result and are forms of life to be expected. It may be the greatest good to discuss virtue everyday, as well as those other things of supposed Socratic concern, for the unexamined life is indeed not worth living. But this of which we now speak is the fight for justifiable distinctions of words; and it is this that is not improperly called the first good. It is not initially a search for knowledge of the good that we pursue, which can be unbearably frustrating. (Our disappointment with knowledge of the good is not—as so many wish to say—that it fails to be better than it is (e.g., immune to constant questioning or consistently applicable in conflicting practical contexts), but rather that it fails to make us better than we are, or provide us with a constitution for peace.) Our first effort is to have and preserve meaningful language use and to adhere to its consequences (even if death is finally the result of meaning what we say). The most obvious distinctions and truths are also the most distorted ones. When the hubris of the criminal makes claims of innocence, it is then that innocence may be called upon to justify itself. Our purpose may then be to find out whether innocence, the moment it becomes involved in justified talk and action, can avoid committing murder.

Harm to innocents is just plain evil.

15. The suffering of others enlivens retribution. Instances of harm and acts of violence provide bare demonstrations of the turbulent influence of environment upon sensitive humans. Unless one's very being throbs with the pain, the misery, the despair millions of people are daily made to endure, then one cannot even faintly understand the just indignation that accumulates in a human body, the feverish, surging passion that makes the storm of emotion inevitable. Such cries of torment are placed intellectually forward (at least for a time) in Ivan Karamazov's struggles with his life and

others. "Oh, with my pathetic, earthly, Euclidean mind, I know only that there is suffering, that none are to blame, that all things follow simply and directly one from another, that everything flows and finds its level." He knows the reality of evil and suffering but cannot consent to live by it. What should we care that none are to blame and that I know it with remarkable certainty? We need not such knowledge but retribution, otherwise how can we go on living? And we need retribution not somewhere and sometime in the future but here and now, on earth, so we see it ourselves. In a world of uncompromising grief, there are particular questions that must be asked and that demand answers. Ivan's half-brother Dmitri similarly laments: "No, no, tell me: why are these burnt-out mothers standing here, why are the people poor, why is the wee one poor, why is the steppe bare, why don't they embrace and kiss, why don't they sing joyful songs, why are they blackened with such black misery, why don't they feed the wee one?" Are there any meaningful responses and satisfying answers forthcoming? Can anything help here? Imagine two classes of individuals. One class, not realizing what they are and what they might be, take life as it comes, believe that they are born to be slaves, and content themselves with the little that is given them in exchange for their labor. But there are others, on the contrary, who think, who study, and who, looking about them, discover and sense deeply social iniquities. They see clearly, feel strongly, and suffer at the suffering of others.

16. Sensitivities to evil lead to violence. Many humans of violence were and are impelled to their choice by the tremendous pressure of physical conditions, by the plain evil of existence that makes life unbearable to their sensitive natures. The sight of the brutal battering of innocent victims or of the degrading, character-destroying economic struggles and inequalities furnish the spark that kindles the dynamic force in the overwrought, outraged minds and bodies of extremely sensitive humans. Theirs is violence as reactions to these actions and conditions. Beyond every such forceful act there is a vital cause. It is a violence that must be understood as the product of an overly sensitive social consciousness; but seldom is this properly seen. The person who makes a violent protest against our social and economic iniquities

is viewed by the illiterately detached as an inhuman beast; a cruel, heartless monster whose joy it is to destroy life and let the blood flow; or viewed, at best, as mentally deranged, an irresponsible lunatic. Yet as Goldman and others powerfully suggest, nothing is possibly farther from the truth. This quick and convenient judgment of nonhuman monsters is a gross misreading of many such sensitive and vulnerable individuals. It is their supersensitiveness to the wrongs and injustices surrounding them that compels them to pay aggressively the toll of our social crimes. Such a human is endowed with a strong love of liberty, both egoistic and nonindividualistic, and possessed of great curiosity, an intense desire to know. Their hypersensitivity may express itself as common frustration with how we speak and how others constantly fail to understand us. These traits of distress are supplanted by an ardent love of others, a highly developed moral sensitiveness, a profound sentiment of justice, and imbued with missionary zeal. Their acts are the violent recoil from violence, whether aggressive or repressive; they are the last, desperate struggle of outraged and exasperated human nature for breathing space and life, for meaning and accountability. Their cause lies not in any special conviction but in the depths of that human nature itself. This violence in response to evil is not due simply to the suffering of a child, an innocent, which is repugnant in itself, but to the fact that the suffering is not justified. After all, pain, exile, or confinement is sometimes accepted when dictated by good, common sense, proper medical opinion, or expert's orders. What is missing from the misery of the world, as well as from its moments of happiness, is some principle by which they can be explained or understood, by a few words that can be meaningfully said. The insurrection against evil is a demand for unity, equality, and absolute clarity; it is a seeking of a moral philosophy, a lucid articulation of injustice that answers the rational cravings of human nature. Unhappily, under miserable conditions of life, any vision of the possibility of better things makes the present misery all the more intolerable, and it spurs those who suffer to the most energetic struggles to improve the lot of humans; and if these struggles only immediately result in sharper misery, the outcome is defiant hatred or sheer resignation.

17. Unfeeling indifference and intentional evil produce desperation. Concluding that hope is impossible in the present world of violence and evil is not without justified reasons. A life of derived desperation is the life faced by many. ["The situation is one of pure desperation." "Desperation was all I could feel." "The only responses are those of desperation."] But what is often seen as and called desperation is not always, however, abhorrence or acquiescence. It is rather a judgment reached or a passion unleashed that will not be tolerated. What happens to a person with his or her mind working actively with an excitement of new ideas, with a vision before their eyes of a new hope dawning for toiling and agonizing humans, with the knowledge that their suffering and that of their comrades in misery are not caused by the cruelty of fate but by the injustice of other human beings? These individuals see that the guilt for the countless human homicides and injustices lies upon every man and woman who, intentionally or by cold indifference, helps to keep and support the social conditions of the day. It is the uncontrolled, unjust social conventions and arrangements that drive many a reflective human being to a life of despair and misery. In truth, then, the human who flings her or his whole life into the attempt to protest against the wrongs of their fellow humans, at the cost of their own life, is a saint compared to the active and passive upholders of cruelty and injustice, even if their protests destroy other lives besides their own. A world of human evil cannot any longer be accepted as it is and left unchallenged by the "new man." What is required is a reevaluation of values. A commitment to the violence of change is all that offers hope in such a world for such a person. They act violently not for themselves but for everyone. In a way the person who kills himself or herself in solitude still preserves certain old values because they, apparently, claim no rights over the lives of others; they do not use the enormous power and freedom of action that the decision to die gives. But the so-called extremists kill while being killed. They are incapable of justifying what they found and feel; they conceive of the idea of offering themselves as a justification for their desperation with the world and reaction of violence, and of replying by personal sacrifice to the questions and sufferings they found themselves subjected to

and unable to handle. Murder is then identified with suicide. A life is paid for by another life, and from these sacrifices springs the promise of value.

18. It is not individuals but human nature that is at stake. Violence identifies and demarcates two different species of humans. One kills only once and pays with her or his life. The other justifies thousands of crimes and consents to be rewarded with honors. Whoever accepts death, to pay for a life with a life, no matter what their negations may be, affirms, by doing so, a value that surpasses them. Some exposed to the evils of existence naturally will become violent and will even feel that their violence is social and not antisocial, that in striking when and how they can they are striking not for themselves but for human nature, outraged and violated in their persons and in those of their fellow sufferers. Nothing, it is thought, must be held back in the effort to speak for and save human nature. Given the world as evil, there seems to be little left for the morally sensitive individual than violence. Still, amid the passion and the rubble there are surviving questions that must be asked: Is the sensitivity to suffering and evil only able to find satisfying response and salvation in retribution and violence? Can we identify and coherently talk about another "species" of humans, a nonviolent species? These questions (and their various forms), no matter how meaningful they come to be, seem to offer no hope for those of a hypersensitive nature to evil and violence. How could they do so? What is to be done? Human nature must be preserved and justice achieved whatever the means and cost.

Evil is met by violence and nonviolence.

19. Evil is eliminated or accepted. Placing, as we have, the illogic of harm and the sensitivity to evil side by side brings a reconsideration of both. They stand together incoherently in our thoughts and actions, each asking for primacy. Our nonviolent understanding and violent intolerance of the conditions of existence must be better placed in our strands of reasoning, in the work of our philosophical exercises, if we are to articulate clearly their possibilities and their implications. The contrasting

positions reflectively invite a distinction between epistemological and metaphysical uses of the concept of evil—a distinction, that is to say, between those uses of evil that demand its elimination and those that are resigned to its existence.

20. Evil challenges the rationality of existence. The real world is good, rational, and purposeful. This abstract judgment has tempted us relentlessly. But such an appeal to the general goodness and reasonableness of the universe, to a rational order of life, conflicts with the concrete reality of evil. But why not answer such a difficulty by contending that the nature of evil is presently beyond us, and if or when that is made clear then all will be right and rightly understood? Our previous thoughts and words echo here. We know only that there is suffering, that is a certainty; and even though there may be causes and reasons for such a life, we cannot consent to live with it. If we cannot find a way to address or find retribution for evil, and find it in the here and now, then we cannot live with our deep, surging sensitivities of iniquities and injustice. What do we care that in most cases none are specifically responsible? We need retribution. Without it we will destroy ourselves and others with us. We need action and retribution now, not in some future existence, so that we see it ourselves. But justice nonetheless will come, you say. Be patient and have faith in the rationality of all things; in the end all will be made right. Is it possible, then, that we've suffered so that we, together with our good and evil deeds and many miseries, should be manure for someone else's future achievements? Maybe we can take solace in that way of helping humankind in its development. But if everyone must suffer in order to buy this eternal unity with their suffering, then it must be asked what have the innocents of the world got to do with it? It's quite incomprehensible why *they* should have to suffer, and why *they* should help attain future unity and equality with their suffering. "Everyone and everything will be put in place and taken care of." But this will not settle anything. We hasten to defend ourselves against such reasoning and superstition, and therefore we must absolutely renounce all higher harmony. Whatever the rational ends, they are not worth one little tear of even one tormented, innocent child. Not worth it, because her tears will remain unredeemed. They must be redressed and

compensated; otherwise there can be no rational satisfaction. Can they be redeemed by being avenged in some future everlasting hell? Where is the higher harmony if there is hell? This puts too high a price on the justifying end. We can't afford to pay so much for admission to the Promised Land. Therefore we hasten to return our ticket. "That is rebellion." Rebellion, you say? We don't like hearing such a word. One seemingly cannot live by rebellion, and we want to live. We need hope or something like it if we are to live. "Everything will be explained. In the end all will be made right." Maybe there is good reason to accept such an ideology. But if *this* is what it takes to get eternal bliss, then we say again that we return our ticket. We renounce all higher harmony based on such a design. It is immoral to participate in such a plan. No moral person would accept such. What kind of person am I? How can one live in such a world? These questions truly can bring paralysis of action. But they make evident as well that acts of violence directed at the causes of evil may bring hope, a hope that insensitive and blind beliefs about an indefinite future cannot provide.

21. It is better not to be than to be. Schopenhauer reminds us that ours is basically an existence of suffering. It is a mistake to assume that: we are meant not to suffer, we deserve happiness, we are owed fulfillment of our purposes, that being alive is a good thing. Suffering as a fundamental reality of our existence must not be ignored or overlooked. We must not turn our heads, argues Schopenhauer, from the suffering and evil that make life what it is. In his *The World as Will and Representation*, there are to be found more than three dozen particular instances and uses of the term "evil." These range from those that emphasize a provisional judgment or possible assessment of how a situation is to be understood, to those that stress a firm and categorical sense of the character of life and the world. In the first (uses making a relative or open assessment of reality, the way things might be) are to be found examples like the following: "a propensity for evil," "cannot be infected with evil," "attempt was made to get rid of evil," "avoid the evil," "is anything but an evil." Whereas the second (uses with a finished and firm sense of reality, the way the world has to be) includes "unavoidable evils," "innumerable permanent

evils," "evils that are common to all and inseparable from human life," "the evil that befalls us is inevitable," "unalterably necessary evils." Schopenhauer, no doubt correctly, often finds our talk about and our various uses of "evil" to be confused and unclear. This is, he somewhat more problematically suggests, primarily due to our failure to understand properly the one category of Kant's twelve that remains truly viable, namely, causality. We remain confused about the causal order of things even in a post-Kantian condition of understanding, and Schopenhauer wishes to make this right. We easily, that is, mistake a temporary influence for a primary cause and thereby misunderstand the fundamental place of evil in our lives and in the nature of the world. For Schopenhauer, illusion and deception always threaten our clear understanding. "We saw that the joys certainly lie to the desire in stating that they are a positive good, but that in truth they are only of a negative nature, and only the end of an evil." A life in truth cannot cease to question the goodness of that life.

22. Evil is not faced but hidden. The inescapable evil of our existence, even when soberly considered, is generally left indistinct, unstudied, and falsified in our thoughts and presentations. In writing about evil and the Stoics, Schopenhauer says that in contrast to what we are taught or encouraged to believe "we find none other than the knowledge that the course of the world is entirely independent of our will, and consequently that the evil that befalls us is inevitable." This general condition of the evil of existence is often covered up or left unknown. Our social and educational systems do not rectify the misunderstanding; in fact, they promote it. Our metaphysical and ethical education is sadly neglected and controlled. We have not learned in the investigation of the moral life, as the scientists somewhat have in their physical investigations, how to seek and press to the very limits of experience. So we draw our limits well short of anything that reason requires. Rather than being asked or taught to see reality and the evil in it as it is, we are usually offered, especially by religious and political enthusiasts, a manipulating reconstruction of the world and its reasons and causes. Emphasizing and exploiting human's unreflective fears, general allegiances to authority, and refusals to face unpleasant facts, many use metaphysics as a

means not to truth but to the fulfillment of personal ends and for the construction of controlling dogmas. Schopenhauer, unsurprisingly, does not believe authoritarian and fear-based uses of evil are philosophically acceptable or defensible. He, therefore, sharpens our understanding of evil and our uses of the concept through discussions of the basic nature of reality and evil's place in it. An ever-present evil underlies what we see in the world and the ways we act in it. We often mistake the immediate appearances and apparent instances of good for the true reality of evil. Appreciating and understanding this truth and reality was one task Schopenhauer set for himself and something he attempted to teach the rest of us. For him, when we reflectively and philosophically investigate our lives, we must not fail to seek and understand the primary or ruling origins and grounds for our experiences; and Schopenhauer prides himself on seeing and admitting what others have not in such investigations. "Only with me are the evils of the world honestly admitted in all their magnitude; this is possible, because the answer to the question of their origin coincides with the answer to the question of the origin of the world."

23. Evil, as opposed to what? Beyond a respect for the attention and reflections given to the multiple uses of the concept of evil, what is to be said about these remarks and perspectives on evil? After developing some "early" ordinary language philosophy concerns found in Aristotle and Socrates, what is now to be said about the positions Schopenhauer argues? Looking to our left, to the conditions of possibility, we seemingly would not immediately dispute the generalization reached or the kinds (primarily two kinds) of uses or categories that govern Schopenhauer's thought on the issue. Nonetheless, from the conceptual perspective of our philosophical considerations, several questions do come forward. Questions about meanings, limits, and possibilities are put before us. A philosophy that listens closely to language use reminds us that our words and concepts are rule–governed, and to be meaningful they must follow proper criteria of correctness. We must know, for instance, when a mistake has been made if we are to identify meaningful utterance. So we might need to be a bit more reserved here when talking about evil. If all our

discussions of good and evil are ultimately going to be met with something along the lines of "only the end of an evil" or "unalterably necessary evils," then is anything meaningful being said? What is being demarcated and distinguished in such discussion? More boldly, it might be asked, "Evil, as opposed to what?" Simply to repeat "evil" in answer to whatever question is asked—or "god" or "politics," evil is ever-present, god is all, everything is politics—is just to say you wish not to talk meaningfully about the topic anymore, but to presuppose it in whatever talk presents itself. Which is perhaps Schopenhauer's point—but then why keep talking about it for so many pages? Because no one else will confront these limits of our experience and they must not be ignored? Because it is something we easily forget and of which we need to be constantly reminded?

24. Evil stands within the harmony of being. Is not the repeated concern with a causal order, origin, and reality of evil, and with the illusion of good, a use of language that itself is in tension with the human basis and limits of language? Does Schopenhauer not use such talk as a way to try to reach past and appeal outside the human context of meaningful utterance? Has he not leaped away from or beyond the very limits he establishes and uses in criticizing others? Can he mean what he says? Can we meaningfully answer or even ask such questions, his questions, about origins? We must take great care here with the threat of talking "about nothing in particular," of talking out of context, of finding an abstract, ideological context of use and then making all other contexts adhere to it. The sense of disappointment with the world as a place in which to seek the satisfaction of human desire is not the same as a sense of the world as cursed, perhaps at best to be endured, perhaps as a kind of punishment for being human. This sense of existence cursed requires not merely a philosophical perspective but what one might call a religious or ideological perspective—to an appeal beyond the human context. But that is not a viable or coherent stand in our reflections on talk and action. Some of the most important conceptual reminders in ordinary language philosophy involve the conditions that make any talk possible. Is not a threaded order of ourselves and the world needed for Schopenhauer to be able to make the points he

does? We could not say or fail to say what we do, be understood or misunderstood, if there were not some unity or harmony of words and world. Is not the appeal to an origin of evil an appeal to a basic and constant disharmony and distress between our selves and world? But isn't some concordance and agreement needed to make that point? Word and object, humans and world, must stand in some systematic regularity if we are able to succeed and fail at what we do. There is no doubt that Schopenhauer and his kin could reply to these concerns and questions, and we are not trying to unearth definitive criticisms of his (or anyone's) positions on the nature of the world. Instead it is these types of questions that make us aware of what we cannot not know (of the conditions of possibility) and that are paradigmatic of ordinary language philosophy investigations; and it is this (affirmed) thinking that we are pursuing and wishing to clarify. (Replace Schopenhauer with your own authors and instances of talk and ask the same questions and follow the same arguments given here. Listen, for instance, to Thoreau in *Walden*. "Nothing can rightly compel a simple and brave man to a vulgar sadness. While I enjoy the friendship of the seasons I trust that nothing can make life a burden to me." Can the use of "nothing" find justification here? "[If the rain should] cause the seeds to rot in the ground and destroy the potatoes in the low lands, it would still be good for the grass on the uplands, and, being good for the grass, it would be good for me." Yes, but what of those things that are "just plain evil"? What of the habit of brutality and dead moral sense voiced in Dostoevsky's *House of the Dead*?) Concerns with our common inheritance of language result in our constantly asking questions about limits and what we say when and what we presuppose when we talk and act. There is no need to pursue these sets of questions more extensively now. Their very asking indicates some of the recurring problems with past efforts often found by such a philosophy as we practice it here. The questions themselves show a sense of what our reflections and philosophy consider important and how they conceptually do their work. They are reminders of the concordance of word and world.

25. The empirical data of evil restricts generalizations. If we now look to our right, to the consequences and entanglements of

language, it may serve us well to read patiently through some of the data of evil and to think about the contexts of use and misuse in which they are and can be found. [he is evil an evil thing expose the evil can only be called evil evil pure and simple pretending to be evil evil intent in love with evil evil that lay ahead there was no evil on her part evil incarnate pure evil almost evil evil eye fall into evil hands a new evil to face evil actions beyond evil looks evil evil expression nothing but evil it can only be characterized as evil that was a real evil evil through and through until evil overtakes him an evil in me denies evil becomes evil just plain evil affirms evil creates evil destroys evil greatest evil of all lesser evil an evil move follow an evil path music promotes evil that is unbelievably evil fight evil attack evil express evil evil odor evil doer evil impulse evil reputation evil temper evil institution evil doing evil minded evil that was hidden it will be evil it was evil it is evil she made an evil decision take something good and make it evil such pain is evil evil personified a touch of evil is it evil absolute evil lived and died an evil woman obsessed with evil nothing is truly evil pleasantly evil necessary evil find no evil there or anywhere last remaining evil what is evil] It is important not to seek or give a quick explanation for the data but to provide instead a collection of the contexts of use for the specific data. [When and with what purpose and by what conditions of possibility would we say: "they are pretending to be evil" or "it was almost evil" or "that was pleasantly evil"?] Each serious investigation and new generation must discover empirically the world through its own eyes and efforts rather than through the eyes of its predecessors. Categorizing and speculating too hastily or solely on what was said yesterday can blind one to the empirical, linguistic facts.

26. Evil can be demarcated. With the empirical particulars as a background, several questions about Schopenhauer's discussions of evil arise. In a rather general or loose sense, it might be asked, could Schopenhauer or how would Schopenhauer, given his generalizations about evil, handle examples and uses of evil like "it can only be characterized as evil!"—which in a clearly identifiable context of use implies and depends for its imperative meaning on allowing that there be some other way for things to be characterized? These kinds of examples are not in short

supply, for instance: (i) the evil that lay ahead, (ii) almost evil, (iii) a new evil to face, (iv) denies/affirms evil, (v) that was a real evil. The data here shows possibly that (i) evil is not everywhere, (ii) is not everything, (iii) can be new, (iv) can be distinguished, (v) some things are not really or a real evil. Schopenhauer, for all of his awareness of different uses of evil, may dismiss much too quickly or overlook these kinds of examples. (He may not pay enough attention to *his own* variety of examples.) Might we not suggest that, in his efforts or maybe haste to reach the claim of a general philosophical misunderstanding of the sufficient reason and the primal cause and place of evil in our lives and the world, he ignores many instances of use that seem properly relevant to his discussion? And what justification would he have for this apparent haste and lack of patience? (This is another typical, one might say unnecessary, reminder of our First Word philosophy, namely, to guard against haste of generalization and inattention to details of use.) Evil is not a univocal concept or without separable and distinguishable uses.

27. A categorical assertion and a disputable judgment breathe in the uses of evil. What is to be usefully said about evil? Having looked from both its conceptual and empirical sides, we view the various conditions of possibility and the multiplicity of language uses involved in the concept of evil as reasons to be hesitant to generalize quickly on its nature. It seems difficult if not incorrect to try to make all the instances of use reducible to one general idea or a priori concept (an error that philosophies with an attention to ordinary language find in philosophers of the past on numerous topics). This is expressed in the idea that there is "a logic to every word we speak." We must give proper attention to each context of use for the topics of concerns we are investigating. We cannot be averse to searching the conditions of possibility and making explicit the data of linguistic use to see what can be found in all that we do and in all that interests us. When that is done with the attention turned to evil, a loose, unclear sensitivity is replaced with articulated propositions that contrast a fixed proclamation and a variable belief. For all of its complexity, the results of our considerations of limits and linguistic constraints do indicate some general understandings and

instances of general use of "evil." There is often identifiable (as the Schopenhauer reflections usefully attest) either a categorical assertion or a disputable judgment involved in the various ways of talking about and dealing with evil. This initial, indefinite (although seemingly heuristically useful) distinction might be pursued a bit further, made a bit more specific and clear. Do we tolerate disagreement or not when we discuss the nature and causes of evil? Is it not often the case that our uses of evil (its linguistic phenomenology) fall into two general categories? They either tolerate or treat as proper disagreements of evaluation and sensitivity to our experiences or they do not. They indicate attempts to end and permit no disagreement or discussion; or they allow and expect further analysis and an open reflection on judgments made. This generalization of two categories of use arises from and finds grounding in the conceptual possibilities and empirical data of evil. For example, uses of evil that likely tolerate no disagreement or further discussion would be: absolute evil, must be called evil, evil pure and simple, nothing but evil, evil incarnate, (maybe) pain is evil. In contrast, those instances that seemingly allow disagreement and intend analysis and judgments to be open would include: an evil thing he did, almost evil, looks evil, pretending to be evil, evil institution, in love with evil, (maybe) pain is evil.

28. Justified action faces a conflict and choice. We now face the opposition and interconnections of a metaphysical, categorical fact and an epistemological, disputable problem. The analysis of both conditions of possibility and empirical data has offered an understanding of evil as either a *fact* or a *problem*. Both characterizations inhabit relatively clearly our meaningful uses of evil. Schopenhauer helpfully began to put such an opposition before our attention. We need only remember his references to the hindrances and conflicts of correctly understanding our lives. He stressed that we must constantly call to mind the fact that suffering is essential to, and inseparable from, life as a whole, and that every desire springs from a need, a want, a suffering, and that every satisfaction is therefore only a pain removed, not a positive happiness brought. We saw in Schopenhauer the claim that the joys certainly lie to the desire in stating that they are a positive

good, but that in truth they are only a negative nature, and only the end of an evil. The metaphysics of the beautiful, he asserts, is also first fully cleared up as a result of his fundamental truths about evil and suffering, and these revelations no longer need to take refuge behind empty words. "Only with me are the evils of the world honestly admitted in all their magnitude." This is possible, because the answer to the question of their origin coincides with the answer to the question of the origin of the world. (This relation of the epistemological and metaphysical is reflected in the various uses of "problem" and "fact." Whereas a fact is "something known to be true or to exist," "something that has occurred," a problem can be "something requiring or in need of a solution," but also "something hard to understand, accomplish, or deal with." Facts are not always "hard to deal or live with," and in talking about a problem of evil that "unlivable" addition to the fact of evil often is being stressed and, therefore, is not always used and meant as a request for a solution.) Epistemological questions about evil stand alongside and are seen in terms of an understanding of the metaphysical origins of evil.

29. Living in the world involves a choice of intolerance or acknowledgment. To better understand the hindrances and possibilities that evil produces, and to clarify the distinction of fact and problem, we might concentrate on a single empirical example like "evil pure and simple," "evil through and through," or "just plain evil." We will restrict ourselves here to the last use. When would we say, when do we say, "It is just plain evil"? What conditions make it possible? Such use seems to require that something confronts us, that something is brought to our attention or is encountered. "It is just plain evil" is often said as a response or reaction, as a forceful claim, to an experience or event. It is a rejoinder sometimes made as a judgment of anger or intolerance. At other times it is a judgment of resignation and acknowledgment. Slavery, genocide, poverty, excruciating pain or death, unrelenting disease, the suffering of children or innocents: These are the kinds of experiences or related particulars of life that can induce the sentence "it is just plain evil." It is an assertion that may be announcing a disconcerting, unacceptable problem that must be resolved or an excruciating fact that

we must live with (if we continue to live). This is to say that several responses are made possible or naturally expected by the claim "it is just plain evil." To generalize provisionally into two categories, "it is just plain evil" can be said with: (a) Passionate emotion (passionate intolerance)—revealing the desire to eliminate the particular event or situation of concern. A call to arms against the causes of human brutality and distress. Slavery and genocide should be eliminated. The suffering of innocents must be fought and eradicated from our lives. These are moral issues that we must combat at all costs. (It is a deep inhaling of breath possessing anger and tenseness.) (b) Resignation and simple acknowledgment (resigned acknowledgment)—indicating the need to accept the fact before us and turn our attention to limiting its effects, a brute recognition of actualities that we can at best restrict. Death and poverty and disease will always be with us. Inexplicable pain and suffering are never to be removed from human life. Although we might reduce their extent, they are facts of life to be faced. They must run their course. (It is a lengthy exhaling of breath accepting the facts with bowed head.) "It is just plain evil" can be seen to exhibit and hold an emotional, strident reaction or a descriptive judgment and sense of resignation. It may indicate our desire to eliminate and fight to eradicate evil and change the conditions of our life. Or it may be a sign of an awareness (acquiescence) of our limits and finitude, of the indisputable fact of evil and of the hope, at best, to reduce the suffering; the need to turn our attention away from the fact and toward the victims. It can be heard as offering a passionate fight against the conditions of existence or as the basic realization that at most we can minimize the harm of these conditions. "It is just plain evil" asks us to concentrate on causes or victims. It presents us with a choice of defiant rage or empathic assistance. (We can, like Ivan Karamazov, epistemologically rage against the world or, like Dmitri, metaphysically accept the world and its evil.) "It is just plain evil" evokes a moral, either/or decision. We are obliged in reply to such a judgment either to make a pronouncement of a defiant, dutiful stand against the world or to emphasize the required need to provide compassionate assistance to the victims in the world. We are faced with a choice of seeing the world (our language) as a problem or an occasion for affirmative expression.

30. Equivocations on "evil" threaten clarity of thought. However one might feel about the ordinary language reflections that have been provided on the nature of evil or on Schopenhauer's sensitivities toward "evil," a result or two can be offered. Given the complexities we have found in these efforts to look a bit more clearly at evil, it might be important to know *which* use or uses of evil is or are directing our talk in any given context. "It is just plain evil." "It is evil through and through." "She made an evil decision." "It is evil pure and simple." When we say such things, are we asserting a fact that we expect others to accept, or are we announcing a tension or situation that is to be questioned and challenged? Are we making a claim or stating a problem? Or are we doing something else (engaging in dark humor or in pedagogical hyperbole)? We must be careful not to ignore the constraints and entanglements of or equivocate the various uses of "evil." We must not disregard the basic phenomenology and logic of evil. Facts seem to stand relatively fixed whereas problems seemingly are to be resolved. These are certainly different and not equivalent uses of evil. You cannot inhale and exhale at the same time. (Circular breathing is not possible here.) Our philosophical work encourages us to remember that metaphysical acceptance precludes epistemological elimination and that charges of moral indifference are answered with those of wasted, arrogant efforts.

31. Evil shows how we stand in the world. "Evil" is a word whose various uses indicate, establish, or identify our stance or way of standing in the world and to others in a fairly direct way. Reflections on our use of it can give us a sense of self we may or may not have understood or of which we may not have been aware. ["I guess I am less of a moral activist than I thought." "It seems I have ethical demands about the world that I was not aware of or clearly understanding." "I am much more resigned to our plight than I imagined."] How do we and how are we asking ourselves and others to live in the world? How do we educate or provoke others and ourselves (on evil)? Do we do so? Evil reveals how we do or might stand and act in the world: *fight* to alter it, *limit*

what it brings, *rebel* against or *acquiesce* to its being. As difficult and painful as it often is to do, reflections on "evil" can help us find part of our place in the world and with others. It is the kind of concept that has that kind of importance.

Violence seeks to solve the problem of evil.

32. The last shall be first and the first last. It is reflective, "reasoned," violence and nonviolence of which we speak, not emotional or undeliberative violence and nonviolence. As we do so think and argue, it would seem almost obvious to say that resistance to tyranny is humanity's highest ideal and virtue. So long as tyranny exists, in whatever form, a person's deepest aspiration is and must be to resist, as inevitably as it is to breathe. Tyranny locks one down and makes the individual a separate and distant other to the oppressor. (Beauvoir has helped us better understand this.) It thereby insults our deepest sensitivities about humanity and seemingly leaves no options for rational reply. There is no place here for genuine compromise, tolerance, and discussion. The dictators of life see to that fact, since no group ever sets itself up as the One without at once setting up the Other over and against its "superior" judgmental self. In so doing, the way in which questions are put, the points of view assumed, the forms of life valued, presuppose and express these decisions of tyrannical interest. It makes it unnecessary, that is, to clarify and specify at each turn such words as superior, inferior, better, worse, true, false since that is now taken care of by the One. This dualism of subjugation offends our very being and must be fought. Violence, in such causes and acts of resistance, cures the individual, returns them to a state of all possibilities (everything is once again possible), a no-thingness, and allows a re-creating of self and world to proceed in a healthful and moral fashion. The battle cry of the innocent and oppressed is: The last shall be first and the first last. This must be the guiding principle and policy of any good-seeking society or any revolution or revolutionary.

33. Violence aims to change the daily order. The use of violence against the weak, ill prepared, and unsuspecting is not only an effort to keep enslaved individuals imprisoned and at

arm's length, but it seeks also to dehumanize them. Everything is done to break individuals down, to wipe out their traditions, to substitute language, and to destroy culture. (Fanon and Sartre have marked these trails well.) Every day more and more will be forgotten by the injured, until they are not what they once were. The violence of the oppressor soon becomes the violence of the innocent, who will make it their own. The assailants find that their violence is now returned to them, as if they were fighting themselves. A ritual of disorder and reworking of routines is necessitated and followed. For if the last shall be first, this will only come to pass after a murderous and decisive struggle between the two protagonists. That affirmed intention to place the last at the head of things can triumph only if all means are used to turn the scale, including, of course, the means of violence. A new day must dawn and a new path must be walked. You will begin to lose your way. After a few steps in the darkness of violence that you brought, "You will see strangers gathered around a fire; come close, and listen, for they are talking of the destiny they will mete out to your trading centers and to the hired soldiers who defend them." They will see you, perhaps, as the midday sun is strong and illuminating, but they will go on talking among themselves, without even lowering their voices. Your language and theirs do not cross. A shared existence is no longer sought or tolerated. To work means to work for your death, to destroy you, the bringer of violence. It is understandable that in this atmosphere, "normal life" becomes quite simply impossible. Our common, controlled life of repetition and predictable variation cannot continue. Violence is rejection of the daily stability and its customs and habits—a refutation of that so prized by those so weak.

34. All suffering, all misery, all ills result from the evil of submission. Pacifists and legalists and traditional moralists are in fact partisans of order and tyranny. On the specific question of violence they are ambiguous. They are violent in their words but limited, conservative reformists in their attitudes and actions. They cannot mean what they say. Nonviolence is an attempt to settle the problem of evil around a sturdy table of honorable discussion, before any regrettable act has been performed or irreparable gesture made, before any blood has been shed. It is the

idea of compromise. All those saints who have turned the other cheek, who have forgiven trespasses against them, and who have been spat on and insulted without shrinking are studied and held up as examples of virtue. In reality it is the violent revolutionary who is the hero. All those speeches of the nonviolent are just collections of dead words from dead languages (they might as well be speaking ancient Greek); those values that seemed to uplift the soul are revealed as worthless, simply because they have nothing to do with the material, daily conflicts in which the people are engaged. Concrete existence will be given an intellectual form and new meaning through the logic and ideology of violence. Illuminated by violence, the consciousness of the people rebels against any pacification. Violent criminals light the way for the people, generate the strategies for action, and become heroes. By this mad fury, by this tortured bitterness, by their ever-present desire to kill those who would kill them, by the permanent tensing of powerful muscles that they are afraid to relax, they become humans. If violence began this very evening and if exploitation and oppression had never existed on the earth, perhaps the slogans of nonviolence might end the quarrel. But if (as is the case) whole regimes, including your nonviolent ideas, are conditioned by a thousand-year-old oppression, your passivity serves only to place you in the ranks of the oppressors.

35. At the level of individuals, violence is a cleansing force. For the innocent person violence against tyranny infuses their character with positive and creative qualities, because it constitutes their only truly meaningful work. This practice of violence, furthermore, binds the oppressed together as a whole. Each is a link in the chain of reaction; each individual being a part of a great living organism of violence; a violence that has arisen in reaction to the oppressor's aggression and bloodshed. Irrepressible violence is neither sound and fury, nor the resurrection of savage instincts, nor even the effect of deep resentments: It is humans re-creating themselves. Fanon never tires of reminding us of such facts. "The native cures himself of colonial neurosis by thrusting out the settler through force of arms. When his rage boils over, he rediscovers his lost innocence and he comes to know himself in that he himself creates his self." Violence cleanses us of a nature

forced on us, returns us to subjective, no-thing existence, and makes all things possible once again.

36. Violence has its logic. Violence by particular persons is humans re-creating themselves and healing the wounds it has inflicted and that existence has inflicted on individuals. It liberates and allows for a new human and a new history. It alters basic consciousness and awakens a new way of being. The revolutionary's weapon of violence is the proof of his or her humanity. Through violence the oppressed unearth equality. They discover that their life, their breath, their beating heart are the same as those of the oppressor. They find out that the settler's skin is not of any more value than a native's skin; and it must be said that this discovery shakes the world in a very necessary manner. There is no consideration of a return to Nature or finding our true, natural (nonsocial) *simple* self. Simplicity and truth eliminate theft and robbery? That is empty pacification speaking. It is instead plainly a very concrete question of not dragging humans toward mutilation, of not imposing upon the natural, reactive rhythms of life, of no longer following what others have given us. We must turn over a new leaf. We must work out new concepts, and try to set afoot a new human, a new species of life. We must use language to our benefit rather than let others use it for theirs and against us. The innocent are not speaking the same language as oppression. The oppressed innocent's challenge to the world of evil and violence is not a rational confrontation of points of view. However, they will recover from violence because violence can heal the wounds it has inflicted. Violence can heal? Yes. That is the conclusion that our argument makes clear. We make (create, re-create) ourselves or are made (created, re-created) by others. Our being is not fixed or unalterable and given a priori to us. Institutions of violence (whether it be slavery, colonialism, government, armed forces, private property) subjugate our nature to others, make us them. We respond to such efforts either with violence or nonviolence. Nonviolence is a passive acceptance and compromise of the situation, within the system of violence. It only deepens the subjugation. Only through complete disorder, violent action, will our enslavement be removed. Therefore on the level of the individual violence is a necessary, positive, creative

power; it is a cleansing force. It is a return to equality with all possibilities regained. Violence returns our purity and innocence and nothingness to us. Violence is a virtue.

37. Violence and deceit are necessary to make the world better. Decide for yourself who is right as the Grand Inquisitor rebukes us: You who go into the world empty-handed with a promise of freedom and nonviolence, which the oppressed in their intellectual simplicity and irrational turmoil cannot even comprehend, or us who give them bread and words of comfort and hope. Feed them first, then ask reason and virtue of them. Feed them even when you cannot love or respect them. How can this be done with so little regard or care for others? It is possible to love one's neighbor abstractly, and even occasionally from a distance, but hardly ever up close. Love in ideology is not love in the concrete. Recognize this truth and you can reduce and shorten people's suffering. But you do not. You ask people to give what they cannot. Humans are forever incapable of being free, because they are feeble, depraved, and constantly confused. It is true that thousands may follow you (and this is what helps deceive you) but what becomes of the millions and tens of millions who will not be strong enough to forgo earthly bread for the sake of the heavenly? The weak are dear to us. They are degenerate and rebellious, but in the end it is they who will become obedient and follow us. Humans are deeply superstitious and flee the ordinary in pursuit of the hidden and the simple. They seek to bow down before that which is indisputable. They want that which is universal to worship. To achieve this we shall say to them, or if you like, we will lie to them and claim that we are obedient to you and seek to rule in the name of your ideas. We shall and must deceive them, for we will not allow your false ideas to guide us. This deceit will constitute our suffering, for we shall have to lie. But in so doing evil and suffering will be reduced. This is what you rejected in the name of meaningful language and morality and freedom. You "truth-seekers" do nothing to improve the world or help its inhabitants.

38. Violence patiently seeks the eradication of suffering. Our work is still in its beginnings, but it has begun. There is still long to wait before its completion, and the earth still has much

to suffer, but we shall accomplish our goal of alleviating human suffering; and we shall be kings (using the swords of Caesar and Europe), and then, after such accomplishments, we shall think about the universal happiness of a free humankind. But let's be forthright: We do not believe that the enormous effort, which the underdeveloped peoples are called upon to make by their leaders, by us, will give easily or quickly the desired results. Even if conditions of life and work are radically modified, centuries will be needed to humanize this world. And in that time who shall possess humankind if not those who possess their conscience and give them their bread? "Though He slay me, yet will I trust in Him." So we take Caesar's sword, and in taking it, of course we reject you and follow the logic of violence. Yes, it will take time. But time is on our side. How many among those chosen ones will finally grow tired of waiting for you? There will be among your chosen ones, sufferers who are tormented by the great sadness of existence, who finally love humankind more than you. Those of a hypersensitive nature who love humankind and suddenly open their eyes to the truths we announce. Will people not see that there is no great moral worth in achieving perfection of the soul and freedom of the will only to become convinced, at the same time, that millions of God's creatures have been set up only for mockery, that they will never be strong enough to manage their freedom, that from such pitiful rebels nothing can be expected, that it was not for such sheep that the great idealists have their utopian dreams. Such persons of great ideas there most certainly are and they will not wait forever for you. They will finally chose us and suffer in their understandings and deceits. They will chose to live so finally others will not suffer.

39. Nonviolence misunderstands human nature. By what means do we remove our suffering over suffering and find accomplishment in our lives? Nonviolent, reflective, prudent action is an answer that frequently is given by "defenders of reason." But weighty, interminable thoughts and passive decisions have failed to change anything of this sort and have proven essentially useless in this regard. Instead it must be done in a sensual fashion, by an act of will. The fate of the hypersensitive person is escaped through a defiant resolve and an extreme truth. Is this to mean

by a passionate commitment to "everything is permitted"? Everything is permitted, is that right; is it this willful ideology you suggest? Yes, perhaps "everything is permitted" is the correct phrase, and I accept such a characterization because you have spoken those words. I do not reject it. Will you renounce me for it? How would you do so given your indecisiveness and flaccid declarations? What will your nonviolent answer be to my proclamations of the goodness of violence and to my changing the world through it? Do you have any reply that is consistent with your nonviolent preaching? ["He stood up, went over to him in silence, and gently kissed him on the lips. Neither could speak for several minutes."] I thank you for that answer; it is strangely stirring, persuasive, and undeniably shakes me to my bones. *But* . . . I will adhere to my life and ideas, for know that I, too, was in the wilderness, and I, too, ate locusts and roots; that I, too, blessed freedom, with which you have blessed humankind, and I, too, was preparing to enter the number of the chosen ones, the number of the strong and mighty. But settling between violence and nonviolence is difficult. It is a moral choice. It is an either/ or that accepts no compromise. So I awoke finally because I did not want to serve falseness and madness. I returned and joined the host of those who have corrected the deeds of the nonviolent. I left the proud and returned to the humble, for the happiness of the humble. Respecting humans so much, you behave as if you have ceased to be compassionate, because you demand too much of humans. Respecting them less, you would demand less of them, and that would be closer to love, for their burden would be lighter. Humans are weak, irrational, and mean. They are perpetrators of evil and suffering. Can it be that you do not know this? That you only speak for the illusive chosen ones? Loving forgiveness, nonviolent acceptance of human behavior, misunderstands human nature and thereby makes the world worse. Nonviolence does nothing to alleviate suffering, and it hinders and obstructs efforts to improve human life.

40. Violence is necessary for a moral existence. Senseless evil permeates existence and is perpetuated and multiplied by weak, bestial, vicious humans who freely inflict suffering on each other. The first goal of any moral being is to alleviate suffering;

all else is self-centered madness. We must not be an accomplice to the world of evil. Freedom of thought and action (indeterminate and uncontrolled "natural" behavior) produces suffering and the oppression of humans. To ease and reduce suffering, the world and humans must be brought under control, fortune and freedom must be restricted. Nonviolence does nothing to alleviate suffering but instead intensifies and adds to it because it encourages freedom, openness, and individuality rather than judgment and control. It encourages forgiveness rather than elimination of evil. Nonviolence obstructs and hinders meaningful efforts at honestly improving life. Violence restricts and controls humans and produces a world that is ordered; it provides the means to make humans happy. Violence eliminates those who hinder the greater good of organizing properly the world. Violence eliminates evil, controls humans, and restricts and reduces human misery. Therefore it must straightforwardly be said that violence is necessary to alleviate suffering, to live morally, and to make the world better.

Nonviolence attempts to accept the fact of evil.

41. Violence and crime are inevitable parts of the complexity of human nature. Social transgressions persist, in part, because the instincts that battle for supremacy in humans are not constant energies in a condition of equilibrium. They are variable forces constantly growing and diminishing. The state and its laws ignore this complexity in favor of simpler claims: an eye for an eye, punishment deters, the sentence must fit the crime. But little is accomplished by such dogmas of stability. In order for capital punishment, for instance, to be really intimidating, human nature would have to be different; it would have to be as unwavering and uniform as the law hopes and envisions a good society and humans to be, as it envisions itself to be. But then, it could properly be said, human nature would be dead. We must think more carefully here than does the state. Since many a motion or action—breathing or eating or working, for example—can be seen to involve violence to some (no matter how small) extent, no action is, therefore, altogether and in all senses harmless or innocent, completely

immune from violence. (Gandhi, among others, has repeatedly brought this to our attention.) The difference between one action and another often lies only in the degree of violence involved in either. A human being may keep perfect nonviolence as his or her ideal and strive to follow it as completely as possible. But no matter how near it she or he reaches, it will be found that some measure of violence is oftentimes unavoidable. Possession of a body like every other possession frequently necessitates some violence, be it judged to be ever so little. We hardly need reminding that the ways we are able to live in a "civilized" society result from the uses of the resources given us and taken from others. Exploitation and homicide are apparently indispensable in our human intercourse. So it is that because most actions today are based on and often lead to violence and destruction, direct or indirect, we cannot justifiably act ["should we do anything at all?"] until we know whether or why we have the right to harm and kill.

42. Arguments for violence allow uncertainty to produce certainty. Fragilities of mind ground decisive acts of conduct. Some say about capital punishment "we may not intimidate all murderers but there is no way of knowing those it has intimidated." Thus the greatest of punishments rests on nothing but an unverifiable possibility. (Camus, beyond all others, has educated us about this.) It ignores the complexity and truths of existence and human nature. Death does not involve degrees or probabilities. It solidifies all things, culpability and the body, in a definitive rigidity. Yet it is administered among us in the name of chance and a calculation. The condemned is rendered lifeless by virtue of all the crimes that might be committed. The most sweeping uncertainty in this case authorizes the most implacable certainty. But we must not forget that capital punishment does at least eliminate the criminal, "the condemned man." Thus it assumes certain persons are irremediable in society. But is there any assurance of this and of the guilty judgment? Mistakes are made, and once the punishment is carried out no one can do anything for the punished. Deciding that a person must have the definitive punishment imposed on her or him is tantamount to deciding that that individual has no chance of making amends and that no mistakes of judgment or fact have occurred. These

are the points, to repeat constantly to ourselves, when the arguments clash blindly and crystallize in a sterile opposition, when indignation rather than reason control our decisions, when an imagined future governs a concrete present.

43. Without absolute innocence, there is no supreme judge. The ideologies of our societies of violence insist on their omniscience. But we have all been mistaken and done wrong in our lives. There are no just people—merely good hearts more or less lacking in justice. Reflective living at least allows us to discover this, and we can only hope to add to the sum of our actions a little good that may counterbalance in part the evil we have added to the world. A life that allows a chance to make amends is the ordinary right of every person, even the worst of person. Without that possibility, moral life is utterly impossible. Governments of every age, with characteristic inconsistency, demonstrate this truth as they constantly claim the moral right to amend what they say are the obvious wrongs committed by others. The identified victims of injustice, to be sure, are often relatively innocent. But can the state that is supposed to represent these victims lay claim to innocence for itself and justify its definitive actions? (Poverty, lack of decent housing, inattention to necessary daily needs are but a few concerns that quickly challenge such an assertion.) Today the number of individuals killed directly by the state has assumed astronomical proportions and immeasurably outnumbers private murders. Our society must now defend itself not so much against the individual as against the state. The mathematical calculations of the ultimate good of violence have changed as well. Today, with nuclear destruction facing us, the certain death of hundreds of millions cannot justify the happiness of the few people of the future who might survive. The witty phrase "let the noble assassins begin" has no meaning now. Those who cause the most blood to flow are the same ones who believe they have right, logic, and history on their side. But without the innocence they meaninglessly assert and give to themselves, they are without justification for their categorical actions—without innocence we must attend to our own failings, not to those of others.

44. Evil is multiplied when the state is the remedy. As for adopting the ways that the state has provided for handling the

evil, there are no such ways. Its very existence is the evil. (Our condition as language users may necessitate recognition of our inviolable social existence, as Aristotle stresses, but this in no way legitimates authority "from above," makes *government* or nations an acceptable, logically defensible, "social" institution. In fact, the inherent evils, necessary decisions from on high, and diminishing of the individual make clear its intrinsic illegitimacy in all forms, whether so-called tyrannical or democratic government.) A person has not every thing to do, but something; and because one cannot do *every thing,* it is not necessary that one should do *something* wrong. The modifications and alterations offered by the state, at best, take too much time, and a person's life will be consumed with nothing but affairs of the state. And with what result? We have other relationships to attend to. (Thoreau has sensitized us to these facts.) We came into this world, not chiefly to make this a good place to live in, but to live in it, be it good or bad. We should be individuals first and subjects afterward. It is not desirable to cultivate a respect for the law, so much as for the right. A familiar and natural result of an undue respect for law is a file of soldiers, marching against their wills, even against their strong common sense and consciences. Backbones replace reason. War is a result of unwarranted reverence for law. (Patriotism finds unhealthy footing here, as Veblen and others would add. Infectious patriotism is useful for breaking the peace, not for keeping it.) We must resist such veneration. Forbidding a person's execution would amount to proclaiming publicly that society and its laws are not unconditional values, that nothing authorizes the state to legislate definitively or to bring about the irreparable. The contagion of state and property is spreading everywhere and, together with it, the disorder of nihilism and the intemperate recourse to absolutes. Thus we must call a spectacular halt to excessive deference for society's commandments and proclaim, in our daily actions and in our principles and associations, that the individual is above the state.

45. Violence leads to more violence when ideology of a state is accepted. Those executed during the Occupation led to those executed at the time of the Liberation, whose friends now dream of revenge. One group kills for a nation or a class that has

been granted divine status (Fanon has usefully enlightened us on this). Another later and in its turn kills for a future society and visionary ideas that have likewise been given godly and infallible standing. Whoever thinks he has omniscience imagines he has omnipotence. (If you don't know everything you cannot kill everything.) Temporal idols demanding an absolute faith tirelessly decree absolute punishments. The dogmas of a state are concerned with the denial of other human beings and with creating enemies and monsters, who alone bear the responsibility of deceit and evil. It is then that we kill with feelings of justification, with heads held high. Such unreflective ideology can be destructive to one's reflective reasons for continuing to live and trying to be just. Nonetheless, however mean and evil your existence, meet it and live it; do not shun it, and destroy it, and call it hard names. Life is not so bad as you and your governments are.

46. The concrete particularity of existence exhibits the truth of nonviolence. The powers of the ordinary, the natural sounds and sights of violence and nonviolence, are not to be underestimated. The proponents of tyranny, the state, realize this and make efforts to diffuse them. They lie and misinform. They disguise the truth, the noise, and the facts. But we must not let this strength of the ordinary be lost or forgotten. Society's "spokesmen" must not be allowed to speak as if any words can be said at any time. They must either talk and kill truthfully or confess that they are not authorized to kill or speak and act for us. The constant performance and implementation of violence, which is readily available for all to view, shows the lies of society and the failings and illogic of reflective, conscious murder. To witness planned killing is to see plainly the reality hidden under the noble phrases with which it is masked. The new murder, far from making amends for the harm done, adds a new blot to the first one. It further scars existence and intensifies the failings of society. To kill for killing is an immeasurably greater punishment and immorality than most original crimes themselves. To be killed by legal sentence is incalculably more terrible than to be killed by individual criminals. A person killed by robbers, stabbed at night, certainly still hopes she or he will be saved until the very last minute. But in state-legalized murder this last hope is

taken away and undermined with social certainties; here there's the sentence, the imprisonment, and the waiting; and the whole torment lies in the forced conviction that there's no escape from the state, and there is hardly greater torment in the world than that. The main thing in state execution is that it's announced and acted on with tyrannical certainty. It is to show the inviolable and unquestionable status of the state and its ideology. Officials, and those who have to talk about state executions, must do so as if they were aware of both its provocative and its shameful aspects, and thus they have made up a sort of ritual language, reducing the concrete act to stereotyped phrases. They strive to refer to it only thorough euphemisms and the language of entertainment. They call the condemned "the interested party" or "the patient" or refer only to a number. We are told of the "audience of witnesses" who observe, corroborate, and review the procedure. We read and hear that the condemned "has paid his debt to society" or that he has "atoned" or that "at five a.m. justice was done." "Things were set straight," "comfort finally given to the victims," "curtain drawn on a wasted life," "burden to society removed," "met his maker," "at last paid for his transgressions." We are to accept such talk without thought, for that is how society does its work here. It follows tradition and feelings and has never bothered to think about the matter. To do otherwise would be to interrupt what is being done and accomplished. The state cannot wait on and does not want clarity; and it will not tolerate interruptions. The temperament grows and spreads. This disposition of avoidance reaches throughout the culture of bloodshed. Society does not mean what it says or want its citizens to do so. However, if people are directly shown the rooms of operation and straps of restraint and machines of death, made to touch the fabric and wood and steel and to hear the sounds of a body shuddering or see the eyes rolling upward into the head or watch a torso falling lifeless, then public imagination, suddenly awakened, will repudiate both the vocabulary and the punishment of rational murder. Habits of tyranny will be challenged and broken. At the minimum, then, if there is a desire to maintain the death penalty, let us be spared the hypocrisy of a justification by false analogy or lying example. Avow simply that it is an emotion, and a particularly violent one, not a rational principle that guides this way of life. Call it by its name, which, for lack of any other nobility, will at least give us the nobility of truth and let us recognize it for what it is essentially: revenge. The particularities and facts of our daily life convey this most directly and counter the lies and ideology of the state. The ordinary must not be allowed to die by the hands of murderers.

47. Premeditated violence, capital punishment, is without justification. Deliberate killing is based on unverifiable principles of "retaliatory justice" and what "might" intimidate or prevent "possible" murders. It degrades humans and perpetuates a circle of hostility. It multiplies actual murders on the hope of avoiding murders that may be. It uses real violence to prevent possible violence. It is intentional, purposeful murder without equal retaliation. It is an emotion, not a principle. Unlike crimes of passion carried out in intense moments (minutes), it is punishment over time (months and years). It presupposes that society and its henchmen (its new murders) are innocent. It produces definitive acts with no amends possible and apology and atonement negated. It is unrealistic and idealistic in embracing the sacred and is without logic in being contradictory. Thus to stand and fight against rational murder and capital punishment is to proclaim that there are no absolute values and to assert the importance of logic over emotion, of the individual over the state, of limits over totality. It is to declare and affirm that nonviolence is not a social policy but an acknowledgment of an ordinary moral life; a living force of action, an expression of one's way of being in the world. It is to say that there is no middle ground between truth and nonviolence, on the one hand, and falsehood and violence on the other. Nonviolence is not a mere strategy of avoidance or temporary assuagement of present difficulties. It is not an effort at political compromise. There is no justification for reflective murder; it is never just to harm another. Nonviolence embodies these conclusions while accepting the fact of a world permeated by evil and struggling logically and morally to live in such a world.

48. Silence is an individual means to answer violence. Our actions and forms of life give words meaning. It is in the context of the things we do that our words are used and have the meanings

they do. To use words and speak is to be part of a shared existence with others. Each word we say opens us and binds us to a world and others over which we have little or no control. Lack of control over what we say provides possibilities for lack of clarity and justification of what we mean. It is in such deficiencies, or rather facts, that are found grounds for harm and violence. This can be disheartening and lead to indifference or desperation. Socrates, after all, talks to understand himself and others and to make clear the nature of virtue. Yet it is a life that often produces hatred and violence. So why speak at all? Can silence rather than argument help with such a life? It is seemingly obvious that actions, not words, express our true values and commitments. Silent actions, better than words, are an expression of what we find important, what we do or want to stand for, of the moral choices we have made. No matter your uncontrolled words, what you truthfully are and believe is found in the life you silently live. Silence, as such, is a moral expression of our way of life; and when it is a kiss of forgiveness or an expression of civil disobedience, when it is an action of ethical conviction it answers violence; it can be a means to awaken a sense of moral shame or sensitivity in another and in oneself. Silence in the midst of evil reminds us that the breath and words and actions of every moment emit virtue and vice, and we must carefully choose the path to follow, the words to speak, and the air that will sustain us. In contexts of conflict, silence is a means of presenting an example to others, a means of provocation, a life of the provocateur. Silence as a distinct way of showing action encourages (allows) others to engage themselves, to have a conversation with themselves, and to confront themselves anew. Silence places before us the difficulties and morality of our talk and action and shows that our quiet desperation may be a "want of expression." But suppose we wait silently and carefully and attend morally to each expression that we and others say, and yet we find with each only more despair, because we and others are not transformed or lastingly made responsible or able to be clear about and mean what we say. Suppose silence only reminds us that our failings and faithlessness to our language repeats our failings and faithlessness to all our shared commitments, to all we do. Is silence thus a rejection of our life and words with others? It can at times certainly seem that this is so, but silence is a component of the fact of language, so where does that leave and lead us? (To merely listening?) It is at least an individual effort to let words go rather than letting violence have our words.

Logic calls for nonviolence not violence.

49. Calculated murder is conscious passion without logic. It is madness to extend the experience of the essentially tragic nature of life into a vendetta against life itself. There is a wisdom that is woe, but there is a woe that is madness. There is irrationality and meaninglessness attached to efforts to connect violence with virtue and creating. Suppose the basic condition of existence is evil. Can we find within it a way of diminishing our actions of violence? Are there acts of re-creating (re-educating) the self that reject violence and contest the connection of violence and re-creation? Does not the effort to hold to meaningful distinctions break the circle of passionate punishment and vengeance? Without the first step of insisting on meaningful distinctions and consistent, objective language use, there can be no lasting combating of evil and violence. There will be no or little resisting the terrible pleasure of revenge. Passions of violence overwhelm unstudied talk and action.

50. The few common words we find in ourselves hold our origins and consequences. From there (the small amount of *our* existence) we must start. We must not deny it from the very beginning. Because every mark counts, the task is to arrive in turn at each of them, as at conclusions. Words engulf us and we fight for our bearings and an ability to keep to a course and to move in natural paths from one point to any other. But where is the good in that? Can any good be found in this concrete, particular, repetitive existence? Isn't anything we do prone to be violent? We have seen that nonviolence, our first conclusion, lay in meaningful, context-based distinctions, our first good. Our philosophy suggests boldly embracing and, where necessary, recovering this first good; adhering to this critique of importance by making concrete, making an existing particular context of use for, that greater than ourselves, for words not my own. If you look carefully and broadly

at human life, you will see that our daily life is one of peace. This state of nature has the law of language to govern it, which obliges every one who speaks. This is often ignored or missed; as some say, "go about doing good," where better it might be said "set about doing good." Doing good is one of the professions that is full. ["I wish to improve the world." "Just improve yourself; that is the only thing you *can* do to better the world."] Few have said this better or taught us better about this than Thoreau. There are, he constantly reminds us, a thousand hacking at the branches of evil to one who is striking at the root. Our manners and methods have been corrupted by communication with saints. Let us first be as simple and well as Nature. Let us spend one day as deliberately as Nature, and not be thrown off the path by the obstacles placed there by the hubris of those who are sure that they know. Let us read the dictionary not with quick glances, fixed purposes, and tongues wagging but preferably from cover to cover. To live deliberately would be to settle, to let ourselves clarify, and find our footing. Is it not the case that what so often saddens the good-doer is not his or her sympathy or oversensitivity with the misery they find but rather, no matter how innocent they be, that they are stopped by their own private ailing? Is it not their clear sense of their own limitations and inabilities that brings their efforts to a halt? I wish to speak most certainly of myself. Many of my actions are intertwined with violence seemingly never to be unraveled. After some soul-searching, however, I can testify that among my numerous weaknesses and restrictions I have seldom discovered that most widespread failing: greed—the true cancer of societies and doctrines. I take no credit for so fortunate an immunity. I owe it, first of all, to my earliest family, who lacked almost everything and envied practically nothing. Merely by their silence, their reserve, their natural sober pride, my elders, who did not even know how to read, taught me the most valuable and enduring lessons. They taught me to be careful and unpossessing in what I say and in what I do.

51. We couldn't live as we do without a daily, ordinary peace. What strikes us in the midst of polemics, threats, and outbursts of violence is the good of most humans. It is part of the background of our existence that there be peace and repetitive

stillness; and thus you cannot bring yourself or others to such a condition—unlike nonviolence and violence, there is no path or advancement toward it. You can only lead yourself and your neighbors back to some place or other where it can be properly appreciated and its possibilities clarified. What we do is bring words back from their ideological clamoring and use to their everyday place of peace and silence. This talk of the agreement and concordance of life and freedom from strife does not make them something beyond the fact of language; rather it is another description of the ordinary, of that which makes the conditions of our talk and action possible. We must be careful not to replace the ordinary with that it makes possible. We are not, for instance, to judge the ordinary as a violent place as so many (Nietzsche, Veblen) at one time or another have done. (Although it may in a case or two be more correct to say that they saw humans and the ordinary as endowed with peaceful instincts and a quiet existence that had been overlaid with warlike and violent institutions.) What we have destroyed or wish to destroy is what the ordinary has made possible. We are now clearing up the ground of language on which our destructions stand. Similarly, nonviolence is not something of the essence of the ordinary but that which is logically derived from such a beginning. Peace and agreement of word and world are not to be judged as the only or even the most important perspective of the ordinary (such judgments would seemingly have to be made out of context and thus "hang in the air" waiting for a context of sensible use), as many other conceptual understandings of nonintentional, brute particulars can be and are yet to be described. Much more, which we must come to acknowledge and appreciate and in terms of which we must learn to live, can be said and will be offered to us in finding appropriate descriptions of the ordinary. Still, the tranquility and freedom from disturbance and the quiet of existence must not be forgotten in many of our reflections and questions. What is it, then, that is distinguished in the ordinary? Is it good and evil? No, our descriptions and reminders of conditions of possibility can only bring us up to the point where the choice between the evil and the good acquire significance for us. They make possible, for example, distinctions between violence and nonviolence, or between the true and the false. But in the first instance, the ordinary does not offer the choice between the reality of good and evil. It denotes rather the conditions of possibility whereby one distinguishes moral concepts and talk or does not do so. The ordinary is our common peace and, as we might now say, it is good and evil. It is pursuits of the hidden and private that attempt to escape the moral (good and evil). The ordinary is the facing of the moral.

52. There are means that cannot be excused. A prisoner is obedient and submissive up to a certain point, but there is a limit that must not be transgressed. It took us all this time to find out (at least to write out and ask coherently) if we have the right to kill humans, if we are allowed to add to the frightful misery of this world. Those who *know* what is to be done or what is to be thought or said deride this paralysis of action (the lengthy time of reflection) and this intolerable anguish. But it is better, instead of mocking or lamenting it, to try to understand and clarify this lasting torment, to see what it means, to explain its near-total condemnation of a world that provokes it, and to extract what little hope there is contained within it. Our concern with the justice of speech becomes a search for a justice of the peace. Toward that end, we have had to repeat the conclusion that all existing states are badly governed and the condition of their laws practically incurable, without some miraculous remedy and the assistance of fortune; and we were allowed to say, in consistency with our philosophy and from its perspective, that it is possible to talk clearly about the nature of nonviolence and maybe even justice, either in the state or in the individual. It is now time (once again) to understand that the ills of the human race will never end until either those who are sincerely and truly lovers of such "wisdom" are heard or those ideologues who have not listened turn to such understanding and ways of living. Philosophy of such temperament encourages our looking from below, not from on high. It struggles to use and to hold on to the ordinary language of our talk and of our reflections on the grounds of our being—of word and world. It is looking beneath our feet rather than over our heads for satisfaction and guidance. It is to suggest that we stick to the systematic order or grammar and worldboundness of

language in our pursuits of violence and evil, and in their placement in our lives and contexts of use. Our philosophy reminds
us of what is justifiable and what is not.

53. Violence is confronted with the fact of language. Our
philosophy fights for justified distinctions, those differences that
are as important as our thoughts and world—and as humans
themselves. We are fighting for the distinction between sacrifice
and mysticism, between rebellion and violence, between strength
and cruelty, for the conditions of possibility for the sensible and
the nonsensible, for the distinction between the human of finitude, often disdained, and the omnipotent gods, which so many
revere and abuse. (We are often accused of using language and
long parentheses to avoid the serious issues of life. Living with
those who know without qualification is the longest parenthesis
we have known.) You think and have said that we just passively
accept the suffering that surrounds us. We are cowards who do
not fight. Silence means consent, you repeat and repeat. But you
are wrong. We do resist, and we do not believe that silence is so
easily defined or that listening is inaction. We desperately fight
for (we try to learn to listen for) the tenuous differences between
meaning and saying, innocence and murder, without adding to
the frightful misery, lies, fury, and violence of the world—that
is a philosophical exercise demanded by a trust in words. You
always distrusted words. "What is truth?" you used to ask. To be
sure we may not know or be able to articulate its properties, but
at least we know what falsehood is; that is what you have taught
us. "What is life?" you later have mockingly posed? We know its
adverse, which is murder. "What is human?" you now cannot help
but skeptically ask. There we stop you and your nihilistic musings,
for we do seemingly have something to say here. Being human
is perhaps the power to grant being human. And it is aspiring to
being human. It is the force that ultimately cancels all tyrants and
gods. She or he that is human is the force of evidence. Is it not
time you ceased playing with words and made an effort to listen
to others rather than just seeing and categorizing them? We must,
however, stop such emotionally tinged talk and replies. This is
not the place for indignation, and if nothing had any meaning
you would be right. But there is something that still has meaning.

How is it that you and we can disagree about this? Is it merely that we didn't give the same meaning to the same words? No! We find necessities that you do not, restrictions and constraints that you treat as open to your own choices and alterations.

54. Privileged authority leads to violence, injustice, and murder. Careful attention to words and language uses are the beginning of salvation from these scourges of existence. We need days of clarity, or at least a few moments of lucidity. If harm of another and injustice are bad for the rebel, it is not because they contradict an eternal idea of goodness or justice but because they perpetuate the silent hostility that separates the oppressor from the oppressed. They kill the small part of existence that can be realized on this earth through the mutual understanding of humans. Similarly, those who lie shut themselves off from other humans, so deceit and falsehood are proscribed for just and ordinary lives. The same is to be said of murder and violence, which impose definitive silence. The mutual understanding and communication discovered by rebellion and language considerations can survive only in the free exchange of conversation. (It is worth repeating that the language peculiar to totalitarian doctrines is always a scholastic or administrative language.) Of course, you and others will disagree. Ordinary prudence and reflection are swept away, you say, by a fear or truth too elemental to master rationally, namely, the basic instinctual irrationality and moral indifference of humans. You never believed in the meaning of this world, and you therefore deduced the idea that everything was equivalent and that good and evil could be defined according to one's wishes. You supposed that in the absence of any human or divine system the only values were those of much of the animal world—in other words, violence and cunning. But it is not that simple. Moral bewilderment and irrationality may be facts of our lives and the threat we must, above all others, counter. But that is what we are saying we can do—not with an appeal to mystical moral conscience or controlled social order as such a defense but rather with fighting for the retention of meaningful distinctions. We admit to the facts of ethical insensitivity and "no traces of any moral misgivings at all" in many if not most people. But we answer them with "seeing the world aright" or better with seeing

word and world aright. We continue to believe that this world has no ultimate meaning. But we know that something in it has a desire for meaning, and that is humans; they are beings that insist on having one, those who talk and act and try to mean what they say. This needs to be clearly said and acknowledged; otherwise violence is a decision that cannot be understood or rationally countered.

55. Nihilistic assertions cannot mean what they say. Reasons can now be given for what was once merely a passion. Can it not correctly be said that the beginnings of evil are found in greed, which includes the effort to own language and the use of words? The uses of language get turned around and made empty. "Everything is permitted" and that's that! It's all very nice; only if one wants to swindle, why, we wonder, should one need the sanction of truth? Why do you want a moral sanction for your saying and doing? If you are going to break all the rules, why do you want the stamp of righteousness? If violence, then why goodness and healing? If we believe in nothing—if nothing has any meaning and if we affirm no values whatsoever—then everything is possible and nothing has any importance. There is no pro or con: The murderer is neither right nor wrong. We are free to stoke the crematory fires or to devote ourselves to the care of the diseased and infirm. Evil and virtue are mere chance or caprice. Your reasoning attempts to say that because we have no higher values to guide our behavior, then our aim will be immediate efficacy. Because nothing is either true or false, good or bad, our guiding principle will be to demonstrate that we are efficient—in other words, the strongest. Thus, whatever way we turn in our abyss of negation and nihilism, murder has its warranted position. If an age admits that murder has its justifications, it is because of this indifference to life and language, which is the mark of nihilism. But we cannot allow ourselves to forget that we must at least believe in our proclamations and protests, in our language of violence and revolution, in our assertions that "everything is permitted," "there is no truth or falseness," "killing is a virtue," "we are innocent," "we are omniscient," and "violence is a cleansing force."

56. Violence and nonviolence speak in disagreement. The very proclamations of the elements of violence, its ways

of voicing its being, require the conditions of existence that it seeks to deny and destroy. Nonviolence is the effort to preserve meaningful distinctions, whereas violence is the effort to destroy them. There is an either/or choice that confronts us: violence or nonviolence, anything can be said and made meaningful, or there are limits and restrictions on what can be said and what can be meant. Violence involves and at root is the effort to destroy our grammar, to make language use due not to objective criteria but to individual human choices, immediate social policy, and laws of states. Violence proclaims the truth of nihilism and of no limits. Nonviolence is upheld by the fact that we talk and act. In expressing the language conditions of ordinary and everyday life, one is fighting for objective facts and against violence, lies, and falsehoods. Inherent in the ability to speak meaningfully is the necessity of going wrong, of meaninglessness, of lying. Violence uses these possibilities of failure, mistakes, and deception to proclaim itself, whereas nonviolence is the effort to keep meaningful distinctions of the false and the true, of evil and good, of murder and innocence—of anything and anything else whatsoever.

57. Violence is stopped at its source of language destruction. Our condition is one of confirmed deliberation: Stop lying, stop meaninglessness, and preserve the distinctions of true and false, sensible and senseless, murder and virtue. Embrace nonviolence and follow what language use and logic demand. This proposed, challenging state of affairs can often seem one of agonizing desperation. We are repeatedly tempted to remove confusions and sorrows by embracing dogma and violence and accepting the deep, pulsing instincts and feelings that propel and torment us. Hundreds of thousands of humans swept away in but a blink of an eye. Incomprehensible numbers assassinated at dawn, uncountable bombs exploding in the glare of the midday sun, the terrible walls of prisons illuminated with artificial light, the soil of Asia, the Middle East, and Europe reeking with millions of corpses of its sons and daughters—in the face of that all we now offer is the importance and hopeful acquisition of two or three slight distinctions that may have no other value than to help a few insignificants among us to die more nobly? Where is the humanity, the humanism and reason, in this? We must not hide

from this interrogation. Yes, these questions can constantly seem unanswered and heartbreaking. However, it must not be forgotten that from the enlightened reason and humanitarian idylls of the eighteenth century to the bloodstained gallows and prisons of the twenty-first the way leads directly. The executioners of today, as everyone knows, are often self-proclaimed humanists. Thus we cannot be too wary of the humanitarian ideology in dealing with violence or with a problem such as capital punishment (or any forms of reflective murder). A humanitarian ideology, Camus reminds us, is still an ideology. Inside every revolutionary there prowls a policeman. It is just one more element of proof that world-shattering and heartbreaking speculation about freedom or self-creation are often a cover for social injustice. We should like to repeat that neither an illusion as to the natural goodness of the human being, nor faith in a golden age to come, motivates our opposition to violence and reflective murder. On the contrary, their abolition is necessary because of reasoned pessimism and ordinary realism. It is a matter of acknowledging the conditions of possibility for the particular ways we speak and act. Rather than adopting or embracing the concepts and abstractions of an intuited good or a dispassionate self or a free and good will, it is a perspective and spirit of being that not only extends our interests and responsibilities to all that we say and do ["we are all responsible for everything"] but is derived from the fact of language and allows one to mean what one says. It is based not on a moral conception of rules of duty or calculations of pleasure but on an offer of meaningful conversation, which requires equals and a sense of harmony with others, requires the temperament of compassion—all of which are denied by violence.

58. Violence or nonviolence is the choice. But can we not try to eliminate evil (an evil) *and* help the victims of evil? Can we not do both? Can we not use violence where required and refrain from it when it is counterproductive? Why is it a mutually exclusive choice? Undoubtedly many of us would like to do or assume we can do both. But a questioning of this assessment of options is a point of contention of the investigation of "just plain evil." That is to say, in light of the repeated emphasis on limits and devotion to constraints of use, our thinking reaches

the conclusion that we cannot sensibly do both. Each alone over-whelms our limited, mortal human capacities and excludes the other. You must choose where to give your restricted efforts. You must choose where you stand, as you cannot meaningfully pursue both violence and nonviolence. Against our repeated claims and actions to the contrary, we are reminded, as Dostoevsky suggests (this is part of the greatness of *The Brothers Karamazov* and, as we might note, of Camus's writings as well), that "I do both" is met with: "You cannot mean what you say here." Inconsistency of using evil against evil is an issue that torments such efforts. We cannot sensibly claim violence is a virtue and thereby cannot justifiably act that way. Questions of meaning and logic ring out: How does one help victims by fighting causes? Are the victims secondary to the causes? Do we fight evil with evil or fight evil with good? You must not forget that in so speaking you are in danger of confusing the different uses of evil, equivocating in talk between a general, beyond all contexts, conception of evil and a particular, context-dependent, use of evil. You are likely exhibiting an all too human hubris of knowing the good, where helping future victims rather than present ones is the issue, where tragedy is seen in the finitude of our existence. Our philosophy, on the contrary, finds tragedy in the denial of our finitude and allows that there is no problem of evil to be solved but rather there is a metaphysical fact of evil with which we are to live. To be reconciled to this life remains impossible, but it is long past time to accept it as an accomplished fact. Thus we can assist victims and save as many as we can or we can fight the fact and make efforts to eliminate (particular, if not all) evil. This may never settle easily in our thoughts, but it does not seem without sense.

59. Reflective murder and violence are never justified. They must be rejected as possibilities for a meaningful life. They never have a legitimate basis of talk and action. Our reflections allow that many of our traditional philosophical problems may not be fun-damentally epistemological but fundamentally metaphysical—and not problems at all. Our concern in such cases is not how to know better or explain further the facts but how to be or subsist with them; where metaphysical acceptance precludes epistemological elimination, and acknowledgment of limits disputes arrogance

of wisdom; where an ethic of duty (categorical imperatives) is replaced with an ethic of compassion (seeing word and world threaded aright). The rationale of violence is presented in a circle of nihilism. It is revolution, not rebellion; ideology, not patient self-reflection. It cannot mean what it says. The logic of existence is means, not ends. It is the task of accepting finitude. It is humans making amends and recognizing limits, not hiding in and following definitive, immodest abstractions. The defenders of violence do productively lead us to ask whether there is logic to violence and how we are to speak meaningfully of it or of anything at all. They force the defenders of nonviolence to ask how innocence will justify itself in a world where our very use of the term (and many like it) is challenged and unclear. Our ordinary language philosophy has given us a reply in the objectivity of language and investigations of must we mean what we say. Because we must believe in the protest and the sentences of rebellion, nihilism is impossible, as the protest shows there is value worth trying to preserve. There are means that cannot be excused, words that cannot be changed, if there is a consistency and meaning to the words we speak, if there is logic to what we say. The truth and facts of our lives are revealed not by abstract speculation or ideology but by facing and confronting the ordinary, concrete, and immediate aspects of our lives. Individuals and institutions of violence (societies, states, and individual groups) are cloaked in the meaningless use of language, in lies and linguistic deceit (empty speculations), in the assumption that they are innocent. Without absolute values (without god and the sacred), with only relative, secular, present, common, human existence there can be no justification for definitive, unchangeable actions, no justification for calculated murder and capital punishment. Reflective murder is not an eye for an eye, equal for equal, retaliation of the same for the same. It is premeditative revenge based on unverifiable, meaningless possibilities (speculative ideologies). It is not a just or justifiable way of life.

60. Speaking is restorative. I proclaim that I believe in nothing and argue that everything is permitted, but I cannot doubt the meaning of my proclamation or the inferences and validity or strength of my argument. I must at least believe in my protest and utterances, my actions and talk. Rebellion cannot exist without

the feeling that, somewhere and somehow, one is right. This is to affirm limits. In negation is affirmation. The very moment the slave refuses to obey the humiliating orders of the master, she or he simultaneously rejects the condition of slavery and admits to there being something worth preserving. Without higher values it is necessary that rebellion find its reasons within itself, for it cannot find them elsewhere. It will not, however, stop its reasoning too soon and hastily conclude that all is permitted or that all will ultimately be made clear and right. It will examine itself and its conditions of being, the conditions of language, in order to learn how to act, examine its protest and the conditions that make it possible and the entanglements that follow from it. Patient, rebellious, tolerant self-reflection will define the values that are indispensable to a peaceful world, will seek a declaration of the principles and conditions necessary for a civilization in which humans speak and listen to one another. Humans imbued with and reflective of the possibility of language and meaning will undoubtedly accept fatalistic violence, but they will never accept deliberate murder. They do not seek a world where violence no longer exists (they are not as mad or idealistic as that) but one where bloodshed and murder are no longer legitimatized and valued. Such beings will understand that whatever the irrationalities of life may be, violence is not the only way to respond to evil or the only way to labor to create and re-create existence. Calculated violence has no logical place in our existence, because human life is primarily making amends, without absolute values, governed by a reasoned pessimism and reflections on our shared ordinariness—governed by a Socratic wisdom that we do not know much of what we think we know and thereby are not rationally justified to kill deliberately every or any problematic thing.

❖ *It is never just to harm anyone. (Neither to do wrong nor to return a wrong is ever right.)*

Second Book

Ordinary Silence

This will be our response to evil: to listen to the silence and to make sounds more intensely, more reflectively, more devotedly than ever before.

Contents

- We do and do not talk.
- Repetition and variation identify controlled sound.
- Controlled sound provokes questions of meaning.
- Questions of meaning involve ambiguities and many voices.
- Problems of sound are inseparable from the fact of silence.
- Silence affirms creation.
- Creating by way of the natural silences is an accountable response to evil and violence.
- Evil is justly faced with an affirmation of the silence of the ordinary.

Preliminary Remark

To the words and understandings of the First Book are added further thoughts and writings on evil, silence, and the ordinary, in order to turn ourselves productively around and see what we may have yet failed to see. The music of Cage, in particular, enhances an investigation of the fact of language, of the conditions and implications of nonintentional and restricted sound. Much the same can be said of the work of Bernstein. Through these additions, coupled with our previous work, the basic spirit of this Second Book is expressed. It is that living consistently by way of silence and controlled sound is a justified response to the truth of evil. To create rather than judge is the wager of a life of quiet deliberation. If we listen attentively, perhaps we shall hear, amid the tumult of nature and the uproar of nations and ideologies, the gentle stirring of a good life.

We do and do not talk.

61. The world is silent. It does not talk. In itself, without language, the world and its sounds are not meaningful or reasonable. Its wordless noises and primitive hostilities reverberate constantly across billions of years; we ask for its rationality and purpose, but it remains speechless and resounds inarticulately. As a consequence, the world has been and often can be judged a confounding obstacle engulfed by an insurmountable darkness of silence. Still, we who talk and act desire to know and investigate, and we dedicate great effort to making the world comprehensible and fitting to us. Even bad reasons make for a familiar world, and our craving for meaning and understanding does not relent in the face of unreasonable silence. This desire to know is shown, for instance, in the delight we take in our senses. We like the senses not just for their usefulness but for and in themselves; and sight above the others, for seeing, more easily than any of the other senses, seems to give us knowledge of the things of the world and clarify readily many of the differences among those things. With such a preference, however, we often set ourselves on a single, narrow path of reasoning and living, judging language to be a

collection of nouns that identify and disguise objects; observing that the real world is to be opposed to its appearances and is formidable, hidden, and "dense"—imagining or seeing to what degree a stone is foreign and irreducible to us, with what intensity nature or aspects of it can negate us, and similarly discerning how we ourselves negate the world. We may have then forgotten that some animals that cannot hear sounds are intelligent but do not learn, and those that both hear or distinguish sounds and have memory or reason learn by listening.

62. Words and silence are materially inseparable. This is the fact of language. What we attempt to mean or intend by what we explicitly say might be discovered by analysis of the form of expression, but what is meant by what we say requires understanding how our words are used. Similarly, a withholding of our words can or cannot be placed and used in specific contexts of concern and thereby can or cannot be meant, can succeed or fail to have a meaning. Questions about the meaning of talk in opposition to silence often have seemed unavoidable but unhelpful, abstract, and mystifying. Nonetheless, we may be drawn to ask if silence is meaningful. It might be and has been thought, for instance, that the only coherent attitude based on nonsignification would be silence—which might be a useful understanding if silence, in its turn, were not significant. It has also been suggested that silence itself is defined by and meaningful only in relationship to words, not unlike the way a designated rest in music receives its meaning from the group of notes around it. Silence is thereby treated and considered as an isolated moment of language (a breather or stop between sounds) as we move from word to word, sentence to sentence. But this understanding ignores both important differences within the analogy (the simultaneous soundings and order of expression and hearing of music) and the constantly indivisible relation of words and silence, their braided, material unity. (However hard we try to untie them, each brings the other inevitably with it.) Silence is not in its actual use a concept in material and mutual opposition to speech but one that continually expresses the fact of language. Silence and talk provide conditions for meaningful sound. Speaking and silence (not speaking) make possible significant consequences within our lives, make meaning

what we say or do not say possible. The language of everyday life includes the silences surrounding and inhabiting the possibility of talk. So, questions about saying and withholding words, questions about talk and silence, do not necessitate, as they might seem to do, unhelpful confusions, perpetual perplexities, and loss of meaning in our reflective investigations. They provide, rather, an enhanced understanding for what it is to be a language user.

63. The ordinary background of our life of language is repetition and variation. Our natural, silent intimacy with others is seen concretely in the ordinary rules and criteria of language use. It is criteria and rules of grammar that show our agreements with and inherited acquisitions from others. They show that words are not used once never to be repeated, that words are passed on, that repetition and variation are our conceptual (and factual) background. In this encounter with grammar we discover that which is more than private, narcissistic self-indulgences. This is a moral of Wittgenstein's private language discussion and argument. You cannot use words once never to have them repeated. It is a reminder of the objectivity of language that provides the conditions of possibility for all that we say and do, all that we do not say and do not do. We encounter the communal, the other, in our every utterance and in each silence. To enjoy a thing exclusively is commonly to exclude your self from the true enjoyment of it, to separate the self from others and to create a life of obstacles. Let us improve, then, as Thoreau has admonished us, our opportunities before the evil days come. We must become aware of the fact that, no matter how far we go in search of ourselves as language users (in pursuing self and self-knowledge), we do not find anything special or unique but instead encounter the representative and exemplary of our being, that which is silent and unapproachable, that which is the ordinary. We find repetitive, rule-governed, constrained existence.

64. The fact of evil reduces us to silence. Whereas the problem of evil asks for talk, action, and solutions, silence and the threat of paralysis inhabit the fact of evil. With the overwhelming grief and inexplicableness of life's torments, we are faced with having nothing to say, although we can talk. A loss of control over our words and having sometimes little or few

words further to say is an inevitable part of talk because our words leave us on their saying. Not knowing how to mean or say what we wish confines us, naturally numbs us, brings silence, places the necessity of beginning again before us, and presents a life of quiet desperation. Equally, our being stunned and struck dumb by the reality and questions of evil produces a condition of silence, of idiocy, a not knowing what to say, having nothing to say. (We have seen how little is achieved when the problems are solved by violence and how unstoppable the forces of nature remain whatever our efforts.) Such predicaments push us and others to engage our selves, reflect on and wonder how to talk for our selves and to others. They additionally provide a ground for violence because our lack of control and confusions over what we say make meaningful distinctions that oppose violence all the harder to uphold. Our silence declares our limits of understanding, discovered at the limits of speech, at the conditions of our being language users. It announces again that intimacy of myself and the world that exists before expressions that are true or false, certain or doubtful, justified or illicit. It reminds us that there is no approach to the ordinary, that there are no *other* words to say than the words everyone is saying.

65. Evil is faced with grammar. Our reduction to silence in the face of the fact of evil means that, if we are to continue to pursue rules of action, then possibly the best we can do is to repeat and imitate what has already been done (talk and act once again). We are forced to walk again the paths we have walked before—but now, at least, our past footsteps—our previous questions, confusions, and reflections—will mark our ground. Half the walk is but retracing our steps. We will repeatedly be asked in our silent idiocy to remove the obstructions or to save as many as we can on the roads we journey. But it is no longer, if it ever was, the path that is of primary importance but rather the walking itself, the exercise provided by each step, as opposed to paralysis of action, that gives our efforts their possible worth. It is not a beacon from afar that assures us but the concrete next step we take that is of importance. A step that takes its cue from, does not hide from, the torment, sickness, strangeness, exile, disappointment, boredom, restlessness that can stop us. It is philosophy

with the business of not only the refutation of arguments but also, and finally first, with the task of a critique of importance and authenticity. It is to ask whether we know what is great and interesting to us, to preserve what is important in that we may need to refute. To face the evil that naturally comes our way, we need not a more favorable position for empirical observation or personal investigation of ourselves but instead a different conception of self and others, that is to say, a proper conception of word and world, seeing the world openly entwined with words. As strange as it may first sound, we face evil with language and its grammar, with an objective affirmation of the conditions of talk and action. This requires that we investigate the conditions of the possibility of world and sound. We need to investigate more fully and clearly silence and the fact of language of which it is a component. We need to recognize better the value of the ordinary silence that is and makes our lives. An appreciation of the silence of the ordinary allows rules of action in the face of evil.

Repetition and variation identify controlled sound.

66. The ordinary is a declaration that words are not our own. It is the agreement and harmony of word and world, of our selves with others. Reflection on the ordinary produces recognition of that and those greater than our selves. So we begin again here by admiring our elders (others), which in a way is as close as we can get to "happiness in finitude." (The traditional and present custom, for those of authority, often is to begin and even end by choosing someone or some thing to belittle and to deride.) The passion here, in a sound and word philosophy, is not directed *against* others, no matter their limitations or foibles. It is paradigmatic of ordinary language philosophy to assume that blunders or errors encountered are the result of *our* misreading and misunderstanding. Of course, limitations will be found even with the disposition of the reasonableness of the concerns of others. Goldman, Schoenberg, or Fanon overwhelm us precisely because of their failures, as, some would say, do Austin, Bernstein, or Cavell. Our lives have taught us the importance of language used by others. The people we love have almost always been better and greater than

us. Poverty as we know it taught us not resentment but a certain fidelity and silent tenacity. (For me, the greatest luxury has always coincided with a certain bareness. Where I prefer to live and work (and, what is more unusual, where I would not mind dying) is in a hotel room (or an isolated northern hut). I have never been able to succumb to what is called a life of ownership; such "happiness" bores and terrifies me. I find it completely understandable when I read and hear it argued that "the perpetuation of peace will only be possible with the abrogation of ownership.") If we have ever forgotten our love of and compassion for others, either us or our faults is to blame, not the world we were born into. We feel humility, in our most heartfelt manner, in the presence of the poorest lives or the greatest adventures of the mind. Between the two is a society we find merciless and incoherent because it takes pride in its derision of the ordinary and in its efforts to own its words. Put simply and ahead of full argument, private property as owning language destroys the self because it destroys variation by denying repetition, by denying the objectivity of language and that greater than and which makes possible the self. We counter such a spirit by explicitly using the words of others and thereby announcing unhesitatingly that words are not our own but repetitions and variations of objective facts, of the ordinary.

67. The roots of sound and song are found in nature and word. The particular sensation of sounds is by nature, the effect strongly physical. It is due to the interaction of the different particles of air set in motion by the sounding body and by all its constituent parts. Together with the first utterings (voix), either the first articulations or the first portents were formed, depending on the kind of context or passion that dictated them. Anger, writes Rousseau, wrests from us threatening cries that the tongue and the palate articulate; but the voice of tenderness is gentler: It is modulated by the glottis and becomes a temperate sound. Its accents, however, are more or less frequent, its inflections more or less acute depending on the sentiment that accompanies it. Thus cadence and sounds are born together with syllables: Passion might be imagined to awaken and direct all of the vocal organs to speech and adorns the voice with its full brilliance; thus verse, song, and speech have a common origin. The first speeches were

the first songs. So, at least, concludes Rousseau. Although contrary in many ways to the spirit of ordinary language philosophy, he helpfully voices many of its concerns about word and world. He is not alone in such provocation and pronouncement about origins and conditions of possibility. Bernstein agrees with this general sentiment, stressing that if it is supposed to be true that in the beginning was the Word, then it must have been a sung word. Only singing, only a heightened form of speech, ♪ Let there be ... let there bebeee ... liiight ♪ could have truly caused light to break forth. Listen to Bernstein's further speculations and additions to Rousseau on this subject of the origin of sound and song. He begins by asking us to join him in imagining ourselves a hominid, and to try to feel what a very, very ancient ancestor of ours might have felt and might have been incited to articulate or utter. We are just happily lying there making a few sounds. Mmmm. Then we get hungry: MMM! MMM!—calling our mother's attention to us. And as we open our mouths to receive nourishment—MMM-AAA! lo! We have invented a primal word: "MA," "mother." As our needs intensify, as our hunger and impatience grow, we intensify and prolong our sounds—and—lo and behold!—we are singing. Music is born. The syllable has become a note just by eliminating the glide. Or, to use the technical jargon of our time, the morpheme is rewritten as a pitch-event. Again these ways of thinking, although contrary to important aspects of ordinary language philosophy, open important questions of numerous kinds. Such thought-experiments about the connection of word and song can hardly help but remind us that just as our ability to point usefully allows us to name objects, similarly does our biology of voice make possible our particular expressions and sounds. These imaginings do not direct us beyond but remind us of the unity of word and world.

68. Music is regular vibrations and sound waves that are purposefully varied and systematized. This is one effort at a working (useable) definition for music, namely, repetition and variation of controlled sound. Accordingly, noise is irregular vibrations and uncontrolled sound waves. Controlled sound is natural. It is law-governed sound. The harmonic system of music is nature with human alteration. It is controlled sound altered by

human decisions. Nature does not analyze and separate or divide its harmonics. On the contrary, it exhibits them within the natural sounds and orders we normally hear. If we sit at the piano and play a low C, we may think we are hearing only that tone—a dark, rich bass note—but we are not. We are simultaneously hearing a whole series of higher tones, overtones that are sounding at the same time. Controlled, harmonic sounds are arranged in an order preordained by nature and ruled by universal physical laws. It is a combination of control and freedom that produces the harmonic system of Western music. Biology and physics establish the limits, restrictions, possibilities of use of controlled sound. They underlie and direct the human expression and system of music.

69. Voice and audience introduce questions about division and unity, self and others. Voice might be regarded as that of my self that is heard by others, that which asks recognition from others who may or may not be able adequately to respond. ["gave voice to his desires," "heard a voice," "spoke in a low voice," "lost her voice," "have no voice in the matter."] Audience often can be understood as those others apart from and not my self. Those who are addressed by or are to listen to another. ["assembled audience," "a book's audience," "confront the audience," "audience response," "lack of an audience."] It is worth remembering here Aristotle's contention that it is essential to the idea of social organization that its members speak (voice), speak together in an association (audience) made for the human. Such an understanding of human conversation involves questions about speaking for others and my being spoken for by others. The questions of how we can claim the right to speak for others, for the human, for that greater than myself, sensibly arise from the notions of voice and audience. Unsurprisingly these can be questions of music and controlled sound as well, where audience and voice are often knotted together. Does music allow one to speak to another, to feel as another? Does it allow an audience to hear as another, to experience as the composer experiences? Is music a universal language, that which transcends the differences of humans? Questions of the difficulties or potential of feeling like or as another, about the possibility and impossibility of a universal voice and audience for human association, arise in reflections on music and controlled sound.

70. Music is a revelation of the unity of existence. Why when we play a low C, do we hear all the notes we do? Why do we say we hear these particular notes? Why just those notes and not others? How does the specific biology of voice and ear influence and find a place in the choice of notes that is to speak to and be heard by others? These are but a few of the persistent questions that need some clarification in any efforts to understand controlled sound. In a more specific and historical sense, we are led to wonder and ask why just these particular notes in Mozart or Tchaikovsky or Ives or Schoenberg? Can it be that the musical composer knows how to speak to others as others cannot? Does a right choice of notes connect or overcome our divided natural and social existence? Does a composer express personal feelings through objective harmonic arrangements? Do the composed sounds of music, heard and listened to by an audience, provoke feelings that allow others to feel like the composer might have felt and thereby share the feelings of another? Schopenhauer asked some of these questions and had many of these thoughts about music. But for him music has an even more metaphysical character and importance than these reflections might suggest. Music is, he tells us, an immediate objectification and copy of the primary will and unity of existence. It expresses as intimately as the world itself does the character of all that is—certainly more so than any intellectual efforts that try through ideas to constitute the world of individual things. Therefore music is by no means like the other arts, namely, at best a copy of the essential ideas; rather it is a text of the will itself, of the objectivity that makes the ideas possible. For this reason the effect of music on us is much more powerful and penetrating than is that of the other arts, for these others speak only of the shadows of our existence, but music speaks of its essence. (An echo of the *Republic* is certainly heard here. But we might also consider that it is not only "the other arts" failing that they be removed (thrice-removed) from reality, but also that they often suppose to give us knowledge. "Performers" of any kind who live on the presenting of knowledge are disappointing. We cannot depend on or stake a claim on their knowledge contentions. They are giving but pretensions to rules of action.) The musical composer, says Schopenhauer, reveals the

innermost nature of the world and, unlike other artists, expresses the profoundest wisdom in a language that his or her reasoning faculty does not understand. It is this universality of voice that belongs uniquely to music, and, together with its providing the most precise distinctness and directness that can be given to an audience of others, music can achieve the highest of values; it can be the panacea of all our sorrows. Although certainly not without overstatement and possible loss of contexts of use, such sentiments nonetheless bring questions of sound and language productively forward. They allow us to receive and consider positively the derived, affirmative claim that whether of a single other or of a collective will of nature music is a use of controlled sound that expresses the concord of our being.

71. A repetitive principle gives sound its musical qualities. Repetition, modified in one way or another, is essential to controlled sound of any sort. It is at the source of our lives as language users and is a defining characteristic, as Schoenberg and others have said, of music and the objective Nature of which it is a parallel expression or representation or part. ["It is a pattern that will repeat." "She can repeat it from memory." "History does repeat itself." "I am not, repeat am not, going." "It was a repeat performance." "He will tirelessly repeat the words of others."] Music embodies a notion of repetition and reiteration or replication. Listen, for instance, to the various phrases in the opening material of Beethoven's Sixth Symphony, page after page of apparent repeating of motives and themes. Beethoven repeats sounds as if obsessed. Repeat after repeat after repeat. Why write in such an unoriginal way? It might be proposed that this compulsive repeating on Beethoven's part is related to the programmatic nature of the piece. Throughout the composition there are constant references to the voices of nature (thunderstorms and various birds and babbling brooks) to be heard in its sounds; and the symphony is given (after all) the overall title of *Pastorale*. The profuse repetition could be seen, that is, as a metaphor for the profuse repetitiveness of Nature, the countless reduplication of species, of animals and birds, of flowers and trees—not to mention all the regular patterns of movements of the sun, moon, and stars. But importantly, this suggestion must not let us overlook the fact that not one of

those repeats is an exact or literal repetition. Each one contains some notational variation, or a structural ambiguity, or a change in the dynamics of loud and soft. Within the general (apparent) repetitions is the genius of the piece, are the variations that give it its originality and individuality. Variation is as essential to the sound and music as repetition. What then is variation? ["Prices are subject to variation." "He measured a variation." "The variation was a version of the theme." "That is the ninth variation." "No variation was discernable."] How are we to understand these musical modifications of repetition? Variation is recognizable difference, alteration, modification, change. But it is difference or modification from what? From the repetition. Variation is the act of creating, creating within the repetitions. Variation is always, in one way or another, a manifestation of a principle that might be called the "violation of expectation." What is expected, of course, is repetition—either literal or in the form of an answer, a counterstatement; and when those expectations are violated, you've got a variation. The violation is the variation.

72. Variation is inseparable from repetition. Whether we seek an understanding of the conditions of possibility of our language use or of controlled sound or of traditional musical compositions, we find the importance of variation and repetition to be generally the same. Permanence is knowable only in change of that which exists simultaneously with what is permanent; but also only by means of what is permanent in variation does variation receive the character of change, of the alteration of quality and form in spite of the persistence of matter. Would it make sense to say he did something *different* everyday? That would make no sense. Variation cannot exist without the previously assumed idea or pattern of repetition. It is often the conspicuous absence of the expected repetition, a deletion, that makes a musical surface what it is. The idea of repetition is inherent in music even when the repetition itself is not there at all. The importance of something's "nonbeing," "absence," or "silence" is exhibited in our repetitions and variations, which shape what something is and how it will be understood and known. Thus repetition and variation are materially inseparable. They can only be separated in formal contexts or abstract presentations of thought. Variation and repetition are

inextricably tied to each other; some things change and others do not. Repetition of anything is most extreme when the source material is slight and less when the complexity of material is great or markedly overwhelming. Our craving for simplicity, which emphasizes and increases our need for repetition, allows for claims of an identification of general laws and the basic nature of whatever subject matter is being investigated. Music provides access to this fact and its importance for what we do, to the characteristics and workings of repetition and variation.

Controlled sound provokes questions of meaning.

73. Efforts at meaning what we say are an exercise in rule-governed sound. They provoke questions about the conditions of possibility of such sound. This is seen in the inherent ambiguities and ambiguous uses of words and sounds. Whether we are confronted with multiple meanings that are either deliberate or caused by inexactness of expression, or with obscure or doubtful meanings, we are often faced with a choice of interpretation. "Fighting dogs should be avoided." How are we to proceed here? "Her childlike smile was terrible." "What you see here is what I call blue." What is one to say here? Musical efforts with controlled sound similarly exhibit many voices and possibilities of meaning. Listen to Bernstein on these concerns with ambiguity and transformational possibilities. Some of the simplest expressions of music are presented, he tells us, as a fugue or round with several lines of sound being voiced at once. Here we find something similar to the elementary simultaneous voices occurring in phrases like "dead duck." The last note of the "first word" (as might be played, for instance, by the strings of an orchestra) also functions as the first note of the "second word" (as possibly played by the woodwinds). In music the notes are presented such that there can be a simultaneous sounding that cannot normally happen in ordinary speech. It's as though one said the words "dead duck" with the final "d" of "dead" serving as the initial "d" of "duck": "deaduck." Or, as Wittgenstein might remind us, we can see something differently depending on its context of use. We can see of something that does not itself change: a triangle, a mountain, a sign of direction,

a hole, an object resting on its side. We can see in a drawing a duck or a rabbit, or we can see simultaneously a duck-rabbit. Music offers just these many possibilities routinely and challenges us to decide how to listen (to the strings or to the woodwinds or maybe to both at once). These dual-sounding ambiguities are often treated as sources of the beautiful and thereby are of significant interest to artistic creation. The beauty of ambiguity is in its combination of conflicting emotional attractions—in the contradictory forces of, say, chromaticism and diatonicism operating at the same time. Ambiguity produces a contrast of necessity of structure and freedom of choice. Such soundings enrich our aesthetic response—whether in music, poetry, or painting—by providing more than one way of perceiving the aesthetic content. But the one ambiguity that music can routinely offer us unlike the efforts of many other artistic endeavors is that of contrapuntal syntax, which is the interweaving of two or more melodic lines or musicals strings. Music can present two different versions of the same idea sounding simultaneously. It gives syntactic transformations of the same material happening together. We might say we actually hear two "musics" sounding at once. The complexities of expression and meaning then rapidly grow and develop from such simplicities and combinations. With this growth of many voices comes the inevitable increase in further ambiguity. What are we hearing and what rules are to be followed to understand it? Which sounds are natural and necessary and which contrived? Objective and natural sound offers these questions and ambiguities, provokes choices of interpretation or differences of use.

74. Transformational possibilities of sound convey meaning. Rule-governed, grammatical, musical meanings are generated by a constant stream of transformations and controlled alterations of sound. Such musical meanings are to be understood as the things done in or to the material of music. It is the alterations (uses) of musical material in the general form of repetitions and variations that gives music meaning. The specific repetitions and variations are the ways the sounds are used and are the meanings that can be expressed. But, as Bernstein stresses, these musical meanings, these transformations of sound, are not to be confused with specific feelings or moods that might result, and certainly

not with images or pictorial impressions or stories, in what one may think of or gather from the sounds. Grammatical efforts at meaning are to be contrasted with meanings or uses of sound that are external to these transformations, for example, the programmatical or ideological or abstract symbols that music can convey. Musical meaning is the use given to the intended transformational efforts that repeat and modify sounds in order possibly to express something or convey feeling. Such an understanding indicates an important fact that allows for much of our talk about music. Music possesses a power or voice of expressivity *and* humans have a capacity to respond to it. Musical meanings are generated by a constant stream of transformations, all of which are forms of repetition and variation, of rule-governed alterations and changes. The meaning of music is found in the continuous rule-governed transformations of its material (in the use of its sounds). This constant transforming of sound material brings forward the apparent truth that it is of the nature of music to be ongoing, to be constantly in a state of alteration and flux, to be grounded in time and change. So, for instance, as we approach a full cadence in a Mozart symphony (look at the opening pages of Symphony no. 40, for example), we seem to be arriving at the end of a sentence, but no: On it goes, without a grammatical period, as the cadence is a new episode transformed. As one sound ends, another simultaneous with it is heard. As one resolution is reached, another transformation or alteration is at work. The conditions of possibility for such musical expression rest in the facts, in the necessities and ambiguities, of sound. These realities are expressed each time anything is voiced.

75. Causal explanations are unhelpful in our descriptions of the ordinary. No matter how confusing or unclear musical transformations and their discussions, the reduction of meaning and its related topics to a "simpler" physical talk usually will prove misdirected. Understanding the sense of what we do is not found or aided by understanding how we can or are able to do what we do. We must distinguish the physical "wiring" of something from the uses and applications that result or are possible or consequence from such states of being. Supposing it was found that all our judgments proceeded from our brain. We discovered particular

kinds of mechanism in the brain, formulated general laws, and so forth. One could then presumably show that this sequence of notes produces this particular kind of reaction; it makes a person smile and say, "Oh, how wonderful." Such a discovery might enable us to predict what a particular person would like and dislike. We could calculate these things. The question is whether this is the sort of explanation or discussion we expect or should like to have when we are puzzled about certain, say, aesthetic impressions or ambiguities. For example, "Why do these bars give me such a peculiar impression?" Obviously it isn't this calculation or causal account of reactions we likely want. Or is it? When would it be? They—the calculations—seem to be something hidden, and I am asking for something in plain view. Such puzzlement is closer to being answered or addressed by a description of facts, by an arrangement of certain musical figures, comparing their effect on us. "If we put in this chord it does not have the effect; if we put in this chord it does." It is like trying to find out the criterion for saying the right thing. "What should I say when?" might be answered with the criterion or appeal: "These are the things said in such contexts." "No one would in that situation use that word today." Here you might refer to a dictionary, ask other people, and so on. Similarly, one criterion for questions about musical sound would be that when something was pointed out you were satisfied that is how "we" hear. Suppose someone heard syncopated music played and asked: "What is the queer rhythm that makes me wobble?" One could play certain phrases and she or he would say: "Yes. It is this peculiar rhythm I meant." "It is the sound of the clarinet." "It is the 3 against the 4." On the other hand, if the person didn't agree or understand, "No, that is not what I meant" or "How does a clarinet sound?" this exercise would lead to nothing. The analysis would oscillate between natural science and grammar without resolution. The sort of discussion one is looking for in all this is not a causal explanation, not one corroborated by general statistics as to how people's brains are known to react in a situation. Such explanations are guided by simplicity and abstraction. They do not reflect on the fact of repetition and variation, or on the conditions of possibility. They do not accept the unapproachableness of the ordinary but rather seek an analysis of it. It is the talk and actions of the context of concern that make possible our questions and answers, including those about causes, and why those contexts that we are presently investigating are governed by descriptions of the ordinary rather than causal explanations.

76. The complexity and diversity of the ordinary disrupts our craving for simplicity. You might like to say "it is this chord that matters and nothing else." But you say this mostly because you wish it to be the case. If your explanation is complicated, it is likely disagreeable, especially if you don't have strong feelings about the thing itself. If you truly love the ambiguous sounds and noise that nature and people produce, then the various complications and many voices will not bother you. Tender expression in music isn't to be characterized in the simple terms of degrees of loudness or tempo (any more than a tender facial expression can be described in terms of the distribution of matter in space). In fact, it can't even be explained by reference to a paradigm, for there are countless ways in which the same piece may be played with genuine expression. Perhaps what is not simple but difficult to express and describe is the multiplicity, variety, and complexity of our many uses of language and sound. The conditions of possibility against which whatever we could say and do has meaning are easily forgotten or ignored in our effort to make things simple. Let us not forget that the reasons for human actions are usually incalculably more complicated and diverse than how we tend to explain them later. What we say happened is not what happened. So how do we explain to someone the intricacy of what "understanding music" means? By specifying the images, kinaesthetic sensations, and the like, experienced by someone who understands? Possibly, but more likely it will be by drawing attention to her or his expressive movements, describing what is actually said and done when we experience music. Sometimes it is just a matter of how one plays, or hums, or marks time to the piece that shows they understand it. Someone who understands music will listen differently, from someone who does not. What counts as so listening? Responsiveness and openness perhaps are essential. It is our deeds, our actions, and our use of words that find importance here. It is our ways of affirming the complex

present experience and facts that we are to describe and of which we must provide reminders.

77. Ordinary facts make "why" questions possible. It often happens that we only become aware of the important facts of our particular concerns, if we suppress the question "why?" And then in the course of our investigations these facts can lead us to an understanding or answer to our original subject of conversation. This is something often difficult to teach children, who learn early in their lives that why-questions seem always to have a place in conversations with their elders. Persistent questions of why this and why that, of undisciplined curiosity and wonder, situate and guide many a child's life. But our philosophy is the education of grownups, and it is the facts of the ordinary with which we begin and only by means of them do we find answers to our why-questions. If we did not so react to sound as we do ["it caused me to grit my teeth," "I felt I was in another world," "you have to hear it, words are of no use"] then we would not ask what we do or propose explanations and theories that provide causal understandings for what we do. Our solutions to our problems, our answers to why-questions, must not belie the beginnings that produce our conclusions. We must not forget where we started and the facts from which our questions arise. If our questions are not about causes, then they are apparently about the justification of my doing what I do. If I have exhausted the justifications for my actions I am inclined to say, "This is simply what I do." If I give someone the order "bring me a red flower from the garden," how is she to know what sort of flower to bring, as I have only given her a word? One might suggest she went to look for the red flower carrying a red image in her mind, comparing it with the flowers. But this act of object and object comparison is not what we might think of as a (our) usual way of searching. We go, look about us, walk up to a flower, and pick it—without comparing it to anything. To see this is more likely what happens consider a similar order: "imagine a red flower." You certainly are not tempted here to say that before obeying it we must imagine a red flower. "This is what I do" grounds our questions of justification and allows possible answers that are of importance in our contexts of concern.

78. Repetition and variation describe numerous concepts. Reflections on controlled sound and music bring additional clarification of expressions and ideas that are derived from those of repetition and variation. Beyond the first effort at a usable definition of music (repetition and variation of controlled sound), we have now begun to distinguish and logically demarcate several additional concepts, which can be helpfully added to a definition without loss of clarity in our thoughts or discussions. Our reflections now allow the possibility that music is many, ongoing (continuous), transforming (changing-deleting), overlapping (simultaneous) voices. The ongoing alterations of musical material are what we do, are what is done, in our musical creations and actions. The concepts connected with simultaneity and continuous transformations of intersecting musical substances capture and describe our musical deeds. These conceptual constituents of controlled sound, along with the demonstrated ambiguities and regulated transformations of musical content, allow the proposal that a viable definition of music might be: the many, ongoing, transforming, overlapping voices of controlled sound.

79. Musical creation looks reflectively at its self and constantly seeks reevaluation. The developing definition of music we have set forward can be challenged in a variety of ways. Reflections on the components and implications of the definition produce important questions that must enter the circle of our standard concerns, become part of our efforts to understand controlled sound. For instance: With so many possibilities and voices of sound, how ambiguous or multivoiced can we get before clarity and music itself is lost? How much are we physically able to hear and distinguish? What can the composer assume an audience can hear in the music she or he writes? To understand better what of importance these questions are asking, it is useful to remember how they actually (apparently) arose in Western music and what brought the discipline to its various points of critical concern over its identity. Attention to the history and the conditions of the development and possibility of musical sound aid our understanding of controlled sound. For instance, Western music and its historical sense of itself faced a crisis of tonality and a pursuit of an atonal alternative as it entered the twentieth century. The "tonal" was

generally understood in such struggles as the necessary laws of harmony, with the "atonal" presented essentially as a challenge to that necessity, specifically to the methods of decision that produced answers to what the next note of any sequence could or must be. Music and its composition in the Western tradition explicitly faced questions that threatened its very definitions of itself and of the possibilities of controlled sound.

Questions of meaning involve ambiguities and many voices.

80. A crisis in meaning is produced by too many ambiguities. When ambiguity becomes too great and the choices of use too many, there is a need for a system of controls if meaning is to be managed and systematized. The increasingly vague (whether real or illusory) tonal structures of Western music still had to be contained in a musical structure that controlled the ambiguities, if meaning was to be of traditional importance and a part of what the Western composer sought to provide with his or her composition of notes. In a rebellious piece like *Tristan und Isolde,* all the ambiguities conspire to plunge us into a new dimension of time, seemingly quite different from most anything composed before in Western music. It presents a sense of time that no longer ticks by in an easily countable form. Music is apparently no longer ongoing and continuous. We have, in *Tristan,* one long series of indefinitely slow transformations, variation upon variation of indistinct harmonies, with large openings of no sound or loss of connections between sounds. In the prelude, for instance, the constant lack of tonal resolution makes the passages of silence sound enticingly expectant and uncertain. It is all largely transition. The ear waits for something to fill the space, and the emptiness acquires a seeming substance in and of itself. This new fusion of sound and silence then brings the question of how formless and ambiguous can you get before the clarity and possibility of musical meaning are lost altogether. How big, how chromatically ambiguous, how syntactically overstuffed can something become without collapsing from its own sheer weight? This was the crisis in ambiguity and controlled sound that music in the West inevitably confronted. There was indeed a developing

sense of the exhaustion of a present culture and its creative efforts. There were finally just too many or too few notes, too many inner voices and choices presenting themselves, too many ambiguities and possible meanings.

81. Definitions and rules are introduced to control ambiguity. To address, in part, the question of how free and ambiguous we can get in our meaningful expression of sound, composers—at numerous times in Western music history—introduced and tried new structural arrangements and variations of what had come before. The post-*Tristan* musical world, in particular, was one filled with compositional questions and experiments. Wagner himself continued to explore different possibilities of silence and ambiguity of sound. Compare the strained, yearning silences of the *Tristan* prelude with the tranquil, poised pauses of the prelude to *Parsifal* composed two decades later. Whereas the silences in the former have the quality of timelessness and a reaching into palpable nothingness, the latter come as secure moments for breath, returning to an equipoise of sound and silence from which music can begin once more. Schoenberg, uniquely in all these efforts to think again about music, transformed the whole system of musical sound from an apparent emphasis on objective harmonic laws to that of subjective decisions and freedoms of choice of the composer. Instead of being a transformation of specific content, his effort was an alteration of the entire system. Although admittedly a rather extreme approach, it was felt that nothing else would do because the combinations and variations of musical tones and harmonies had reached an endpoint; without such a large transformation of material no original beauty or new forms of expression were to be discovered. The reaction to such a radical effort was one of derision or liberation, with the expected formation of factions of conflict: nontonal "moderns" (Schoenberg) versus polytonal "neoclassicists" (Stravinsky). Schoenberg's defenders and Stravinsky's detractors stressed that the traditionalists presented misguided criticisms of the new system by assuming that the tonal idiom of the last 350 years had been derived from nature. They conservatively and wrongly believed that to alter and go beyond these firmly established theoretical principles was a violation of absolute law, whereas in

fact transformations of the system had always taken place and must continue as always. (It is inherent in the definition of music that there be such changes.) Furthermore, these ossified principles of the traditionalists are actually nothing but clear evidence of social pressures rather than statements of objective truth. The idea that the tonal system is exclusively of natural origin is an illusion rooted in a false history and metaphysics, said Schoenberg's proponents. The camps of dispute became so greatly divided that they found it difficult to feel that they were even speaking the same language. Every word the others said chagrined one; and there was a sense of not having anything meaningful to say to others who opposed what one thought important about the ways of composing. The disagreements seemed insurmountable. How was one to respond to those to whom no words seemed of any use? For Schoenberg, the answer was to create in the face of the differences—create so as to achieve one convulsive transformation of the tonal system. There must be no looking back. No set of notes was to be given priority any more over others. Immediate repetition and a doubling of notes were to be avoided because this could be interpreted as a root phrase, even a tonic. We must be free to choose the next note. That would be the path to leaving tonality behind. However, the general effect of such composing, at first, was not one of freedom but of a haunted, meandering, rootless (some said "psychotic") presentation of unrestrained, atonal sound. Such atonality cried out for and was in need of a system of control if meaningful expression was to be achieved or was to be of concern. Thus serialism and twelve-tone musical systems were introduced to provide just such regulations. Schoenberg's Opus no. 23, *Five Piano Pieces*, 1923, was to give music this new, significant air to breath. Fresh definitions and rules of note arrangement were established (e.g., no single tone was repeated until all other eleven had been sounded) to control the strongly ambiguous atonal wanderings of those composers who turned away from the hierarchical, tonal musical systems and structures. The new ambiguities were controlled by new definitions and rules of composition.

82. The turning away from the past is a turning toward it. With the creation of the new system of the compositional rules of

serialism, the conflict over what was an artificially created composition and what a natural, necessary product of the harmonies of nature continued and would not cease. The struggle between subjectively planned twelve-tone rows and the so-called natural tonal harmonies raged; it was expressing still the old concerns of ambiguity and freedom that were ever-present in musical composition. For all the consternation and outright hatred that was displayed, however, what was missed in the hostilities was that Schoenberg, *like* Stravinsky and his predecessors, altered and upset the conventional system in order to gain increased expressive power. The bludgeoning efforts of critics like Adorno and others—to find and announce an irreconcilable conflict between good and evil in the new and old approaches to sound and music—caused many to miss this deeper commonality and agreement. Both the Schoenberg and Stravinsky approaches sought new ways to unleash music's powers of expression. For all of serialism's efforts to the contrary, it could not free itself from old desires, questions, and problems. In fact, argues Bernstein and others, tonality haunts those works that try to abandon it. It is an interesting reminder, for instance, that it is, of course, the same twelve notes of tonal harmony and structure, now controlled differently, that give serialism its transformational material. So even when tonality is not there, it places, hovers over, torments the twelve-tone pieces. Music is that which, however changed, derives from the objective tonal laws and facts of nature. It is controlled by tonal limits and restrictions even when it is nontonal. It is a rejection but at the same time an acknowledgment of tonality that fundamentally characterizes serialism; and such effort raises the question whether the turning found in serialism is to be understood as a turning away from the tonal society that demands conformity more than as a turning toward it, as a gesture of confrontation. "It is a turning to something new. The method of composing with twelve tones grew out of necessity. It answered a need for originality and freedom and creativity. All tonal compositions essentially have been done before." Well, yes, and all words have been said before, otherwise they wouldn't be words, parts of a shared language. Whatever our forms of expressions, we cannot escape the conditions of possibility of what we do.

83. The conventional and necessary can be placed in agreement. Examining the unsettled perspective given of the history of Western music, and looking once again at the components of the proposed definition of music—many, ongoing, transforming, overlapping voices of controlled sound—we find questions about which components and aspects of our musical talk, which concepts are necessary and which conventional. Which can withstand the upheavals of change and which cannot? These questions somewhat naturally arise in our present concerns and can be asked usefully in terms of the tensions and connections between planned twelve-tone rows, human subjectivity, and the apparent natural tonal harmonies of objective nature. Additionally a more general concern that presses here is how we stand ... where do we find ourselves in our musical expressions and compositions? We seem to be caught between the rootless and the rooted, the ungrounded and the grounded, the conventional and the necessary. Are humans apart from or a part of the world and nature? Schoenberg's dodecaphonic system answers the need for a new practice of controls, but it still produces a traditional philosophical problem. Is the new system based on factual laws that we have been given by objective nature, the necessary rule-governed relationships that allow for meaning? Or is it an artificial language that is largely form without content and without justifiable rules and meaning? Are we not seemingly pursuing conventional structures at the expense of natural, necessary content in the Schoenberg system of rules? Such questions most certainly can begin to overwhelm and numb us and bring dejection. We can feel as if we have lost our place and no longer have any understanding of how we are to proceed. But the conflict and our "psychotic placement" between modes of expression need not be thought of as inevitably one of despair and disagreement. Berg's Violin Concerto, for instance, as with so many of his compositions, demonstrates and uses this discord and conflict to great and positive effect. His chosen twelve-tone row for the piece contains major, minor, and whole-tone elements. He combines the serialism materials of the composition with purely tonal sounds, with, that is, a Carinthian folksong and a chorale using Bach's harmonization. Creative tension, excitement, and even joy in the ambiguities, multiplicity of

voices, and conflicts of expression can certainly be felt in this last completed composition of Berg. When we talk of convention and necessity we are obliged, we might remind ourselves, not to stop short in our reflections but must find that which makes each possible. What are those conditions of possibility? Our conflicts are based on common forms of life and agreements of language use. Necessity and convention find concordance in efforts to express and describe human (language) nature.

84. What has to be accepted are forms of life. Our thinking about convention usually is—and has been in much of the recent history of Western culture and music—a sense of the arrangements of preference or expediency of a particular group or culture. ["The traffic laws are only convention." "It is just convention that they say that." "That is but a convention for how we do things."] But this need not be our only way of thinking and is not the only way of using the word. Instead of "convention" as mere convenience (only, just, but), we can speak of it in terms of the biology, history, and geography of human existence. ["If you prick us do we not bleed?" "She learned to lie." "I can continue my thought even after that interruption." "If we could not write (sail, divide, defend), then those concerns would have no importance."] We can think of convention as those forms of life that are normal to any group of creatures we call human, any group about which we will say, for example, that they have a past to which they respond, or a geographical environment that they cultivate or manipulate or exploit in certain ways for certain humanly comprehensible motives. ["That is our convention; it is what we do." "To understand the behavior, this convention must be observed." "You cannot do properly the calculations unless you remember and follow this convention."] Here the "conventions" are not variable patterns of life that differentiate human beings from one another but rather the exigencies of conduct and feeling that all humans share. It helps to keep in mind that an important Wittgensteinian reminder is of the depth of convention in human life—a reminder that insists not only on the conventionality of human society but, we could say, on the conventionality of human nature itself. So are we saying that human convention and agreement decide what is true and what is false? No. It is what human

beings *say* that is true and false; they agree in the *language* they use. That is not agreement in alterable conventions or opinions but in form of life. It is not, then, individual choices or necessities (Schoenberg versus Stravinsky) that our present musical reflections attempt to make most prevalent but rather the nature of humans themselves. What we are supplying is not primarily historical remarks on the development of music (challenge or change it as you see fit, and then ask the questions that are asked here) but rather descriptions of the ordinary—descriptions of possibilities given when our specific concern is with controlled sound. We are not contributing curiosities or historical facts about music but rather remarks on the natural condition of human beings. We are providing observations that no one has doubted but that have escaped being said only because they are always before our eyes and in our ears.

85. Old forms hold new content. When confronted with overwhelming confusions and uncontrolled facts of existence, we often must start again in our efforts to understand and live meaningfully in the world and do what we have done before but with our old steps before us. We might breathe life back into our investigations of sound and meaning through a neoclassicism, with what might be called *objective expressivity.* This is a suggestion from, among others, Stravinsky and Bernstein: an effort to use humor, dissonance, conflicting forms of past expression to achieve new perspective. The present text of voices and exercises in ordinary language philosophy—like several labors before it—is not inappropriately judged to be in part a neoclassic philosophy, an effort at objective expressivity. It regards the ordinary, in this context of controlled sound, as the classic, as that which is the remarkably typical (e.g., classic symptoms), and the neoclassic is the modern repetition of the ordinary. Neoclassicism is an attempt to face the numbness and silence that befalls us (exactly that which atonality brought to musical creation for so many) through achieving a more removed perspective on traditional subject-matter, by distancing the failing and struggling self with efforts at extensive description and conceptual reflection of language use.

86. We need and want old words. The self that falls into having nothing to say yet craves expression and sense is given voice

once again through old forms, through repetition and variation; through the ordinary comes the extraordinary. We might ask what this closeness of old and new contexts means, why it exists or would need to exist, especially if philosophy and music, or reflective endeavors in general, are always in revolt against their past, or rather their present. The neoclassical is in the nature of a revival; it answers a need for renewal and is thereby possibly therapeutic. To be classic is to repeat one's self. To be neoclassic is to stress a new reflective clarity and logical awareness in one's repetitions. The development of the romantic symphony in Western music might be viewed usefully as a series of efforts in neoclassicism. Whether it be the symphonies of Berlioz, Schubert, Mendelssohn, Schumann, or Dvorak, the effort to provide an expressive content, a romantic lyricism, through the small melodic units of classical structures, by means of a clear logical coherence and imposing form, is not hard to recognize. Bruckner also constructed great cathedrals of sound in similar ways—but they are (for the most part) unfinished neoclassical monuments whose formalism and rigid symmetry do not always convince the modern mind. They do not easily speak to temperaments that often lack his particular faith in the underlying order of the universe and that face a present existence he seems not equally to face. Mahler's First Symphony, similarly, is an important source in the history of music in this regard, because it not only contains an entire (third) movement based on an old song theme ("Frere Jacques") expressed in a contemporary language, but it is unabashedly plagiaristic. It tends as a result to offend the need in many individuals to have their own voice, to be modern. (Bruckner's compositions are often without a compelling logic, with abrupt pauses and resumptions, whereas Mahler's overpowering urge was to achieve in his music an *expressive clarity,* but this was seemingly lost in the length of his expressions. These may be defects in Bruckner's and Mahler's constructive power of writing or—more likely—a defect in the listener. A contentious stance with the music's pluralism, the cravings of simplicity and ease of understanding, is likely the reason extensive moments of dense sound, quiet ponderousness, high drama, and complete silence lying side by side are difficult for the listener.) This technique of "borrowed objects" is then greatly enhanced and perfected in subsequent compositions and will be released full-blown in the consciously, self-aware neoclassicism that is a crucial mark and effort of many twentieth-century composers, including, importantly, the "later" Schoenberg and Stravinsky. Does it betoken an impoverishment of resources? That in order to mean what we say we must have recourse to what has been used before, to the forms of life of our elders? On the contrary, it reaffirms our shared links with the past, our traditions and roots. Because we demand our own voice, we often disguise that relationship to the past by coating it in our tough fashionable vernacular and expressing it through masks and in flights from the ordinary. We call for and require the deep-rooted words of our elders, but they are transfigured by our present, our unprecedented experience of discovery, displacement, and inhabitation, by the mad conflicts between the desire for freedom and unending disappointment with our failings to become new.

87. To create is to affirm. A conviction in the "Yes" of existence, in a neoclassical affirmation of what we do, cultivates meaningful expression. A trust in the harmony and consistency of being (in, for instance, the oneness and unity of Schopenhauer's notion of will) must accompany what we creatively attempt to do. That solidity and concordance of being are found in multiplicity (in the many voices of existence). The self is the variation of the repetitive, many voices of others, of the expressions of others. The ambiguities of these many voices leave us with confusions and questions rather than lucid understandings and clear answers— leave us with a search for and exploration of the self. It is an investigation, to be sure, of our own being, ourselves, but it is not a concern with personal, private, "inside" being (whatever exactly that is) but rather with expressing the being (the "outside" being) we have in common with others, with acknowledging the repetition of existence, without which there can be no variations, no self. The ordinary, silent harmony of word and world serves as the condition of possibility of controlled sound and of our selves and others, and it is affirmed in efforts at creation. Is there objective expressivity? The words seem mutually exclusive. "Objectivity" (that which is external to the person) and "expression" (a person's

feelings or appearance) seem often to never touch or at best grate against each other in an unhelpful way. Is there a context of use where they can be combined meaningfully? It might be a question of whether we can speak personally to others, find the words or sounds to express ourselves to others. In philosophy, Wittgenstein's discussion of private language might suggest that this is a way to understand what we are trying to do or avoid doing in our reflective exercises. In music, Stravinsky's neoclassicism offers a means that allows us to voice our selves dispassionately to an audience. Are philosophy and art, or meaningful talk, still possible in our centuries of darkness and death? The sense of the absurd and the black, ironic, bitter joke that is often our existence is now to be met with objective, personal expression, with the grammar of our lives. In the face of the fact of evil we must ask what we personally are or can do and say. This reflection on the nature of self, as exemplified in musical expression, is a struggle with sound and freedom and necessity; and what is offered is a neoclassical assertion of "Yes" in opposition to negation, evil, and death. But as so given, it is and remains inarticulate and but a hopeless hope. It does not seem to be something that can be counted on or capable of grounding our choices and actions. How is a creative, affirmative effort meaningfully possible in the face of just plain evil and moral insensitivity? "It is provided through an honest confronting of negation and death." And how exactly is that done? Why should we believe such authenticity is achievable? It is this quiet desperation with existence and its facts of controlled sound that force questions of meaning, beyond simple ambiguities of use, to return. Old questions now find a new place. Is there anything meaningful in a world permeated by death, evil, immorality, and ultimate annihilation? How are we to live given the fact of evil? Affirmations of "a self constrained" need clear articulation and methods of expression.

Problems of sound are inseparable from the fact of silence.

88. Music is the sound and silence of the world. However transformed and varied, music is the resonances and tranquilities of our nature, of our word and world. We could not talk of the

individual sounds we do, or hear particular sounds as certain notes or phrases, if there were not limits and rules of order that identify sound, if there were not ways of distinguishing sound and nonsound. To be any sound, as well as to be different and individual sounds, there must be something from which sounds are demarcated and differentiated. Sound must be dissimilar from something and discernible from something to be what it is. Those limits and nonsounds are sometimes called silence. The conditions of possibility and implications of silence cannot seemingly be ignored in conceptual reflections on controlled sound. The objective facts of sound remind us of the necessity of silence. But certainly we hear and feel transposed by pulsing, invigorating sounds, not by cool, impassioned silences. Isn't that what is important in understanding music? It is certainly true that our musical, subjective experiences can often be overwhelming; we find ourselves filled with great emotions because of particular musical experiences of sounds heard and felt. Surely this is one of music's great attractions. But no matter how irresistible these feelings and encounters, we must not in our more patient reflections forget or flee from the objectivity underlying these subjective expressions and adornments. Music as merely an ornament of our existence is an emptiness of our lives to be resisted, as both Wagner's *Der Ring des Nibelungen* and Cage's *Europeras* show us in their own way. We must let go of the ornamental surface and ask of the possibilities of our existence, the conditions that make possible who and what we are and might be. Music is that derived from the sounds and silences of (the objective laws of) nature. Countless people ignore these objectivities of our existence and thereby never experience the most enjoyable of all music, the sounds that we hear when we are just quiet. Many in our different societies go through each day walking the streets and riding in cars and on buses and sitting in parks and so forth while playing radios and various types of sophisticated audio equipment, with earphones on or off; and they don't hear the world around them. It is as though they fear that the world is uninhabitable—it is as though they find it necessary to flee the ordinary. They cut themselves off from the rich, diverse experience of nature, which is free and edifying. (I sat in my sunny doorway from sunrise till noon, rapt in a reverie, in undisturbed solitude and stillness, while the birds sang around or flitted noiseless through the house, until by the sun falling in at my west window, or the noise of some traveler's wagon on the distant highway, I was reminded of the lapse of time.) The end of music, as some have suggested, may very well be in the technological, commercial reproduction of sound (in prerecorded, digitally downloaded, compact disc, phonographic record collections); however, whatever sense of the end might be proposed, it can properly be said: The world (its sounds and silences) is (the beginning of) music.

89. The empirical data of silence exhibits an objective phenomenon. Examine the following possible uses of silence. [a period of silence maintain silence made a terrible silence sisterly silence silence gives consent suffer in silence fall into silence break his silence conspiracy of silence keep the silence in silence deafening silence put to silence reduce to silence tower of silence grave silence cold silence profound silence time of silence through the silence interrupt the silence continue the silence begin the silence nearing a silence ignore her silence end the silence remember his silence lost the silence lost in silence kept to silence shown by the silence pass over in silence found its silence no silence all silence some silence next to silence listen to the silence ruined the silence disturbing silence restful silence silence the mob silence of the victim deadly silence dead silence beautiful silence withdrew into solemn silence sullen silence silence on both sides] The data makes clear (once again) that the threat of equivocation (here on the word "silence") must be heeded. "Silence" as not speaking, "silence" as an active experience, "silence" as something forgotten are uses that must not be treated equivalently. When and with what purpose and by what conditions of possibility would we say: "She has kept to her silence" or "The silence was so disturbing I had to leave" or "He found a proper level of silence"? A data collection of the uses of "silence" helps prevent hasty generalizations about its nature, which is no small accomplishment. It also, however, allows for (after appropriate work) some tentative thoughts and conclusions about its description and meaning. We might, in light of the data and the conceptual work it engenders, propose that silence is not a conflicting element with what we

hear or that which is in opposition to sound (talk and action).
Rather it might be proposed that it is that plainly and constantly
experienced.

90. Silence opposes controlled sound. Music is brought to
an end by silence. Music stops at identifiable moments and gives
way to silence. That is what is meant by "rest" in music, namely,
an interval of silence of a specific duration. But are the rests that
stop sounds not an essential component of music? The silences
between the asserted notes and tones are certainly part of what
we hear. However, they do seem to be in opposition to music
in that they stop the continuing movement of the sound. So, at
least in this sense, the definition of music that has been offered
needs further examination, as silence introduces an immediate
doubt about the "many," "ongoing," "simultaneous voices." A
consideration of time and timelessness enters our concerns as we
think about silence and controlled sound. Seemingly, music can
at many moments have and seek to have no movement or voices.
Several questions might now be asked: How do we count silence?
If silence is opposed to sound and cannot be heard, then how
do we measure what is not heard? What is meant by silence in
any of these contexts of concern? If it can be counted and stands
alongside or in accordance with sound, then must silence not be
something other than the negation or the absence of sound? In
Debussy's *Prelude to the Afternoon of a Faun,* for instance, we are
challenged, in the opening pages, with a vagueness of key and
then face a bar of silence. "Six slow beats of no music." It is much
like what is found in *Tristan und Isolde,* but it is seemingly even
more ambiguous and uncontrolled. How do we know we have
six beats—that they are six beats? How do we count the silences
in the *Prelude to the Afternoon of a Faun?* What are we counting? This confusion and planned puzzlement with an absence of
sound seem to challenge if not negate tonality and the definition
of music that arises with it. The relations of sound and silence
produce questions seemingly destructive to the understanding
of controlled sound that has first served us. Our definition of
music seems in danger of no longer being generally useable or
too restrictive once no sound is to count. Silence is a problem
that must be solved.

91. Silence is the background of controlled sound. In Ives's 1908 composition *The Unanswered Question* the silences of the world, far from being absences or stopping of sound, are persistently heard. Ives's conception of silence in that masterful work is one of repeated tonal harmonies that provide the background possibilities for hearing dissonances and atonalities. Ives answered the question of the possibility of music, most interestingly, with a concept of silence, with silence understood as a tonal repetition of background sound. Here is Ives's descriptive foreword to the piece. "The strings play pianissimo throughout with no change in tempo. They are to represent 'The Silences of the Druids— Who Know, See and Hear Nothing.' The trumpet intones 'The Perennial Question of Existence,' and states it in the same tone of voice each time." This, then, provides the structure and questions for our hearing. The "hunt for the 'Invisible Answer' undertaken by the flutes and other human beings becomes gradually more active, faster and louder.... [These] 'Fighting Answerers,' as time goes on ... seem to realize a futility and begin to mock 'The Question'—the strife is over for the moment. After they disappear, 'The Question' is asked for the last time, and 'The Silences' are heard beyond in 'Undisturbed Solitude.'" Although Ives gives a metaphysical reading to the piece, Bernstein sees it providing a strictly musical question, namely, the question of "Whither Music?" Bernstein's description of Ives's *The Unanswered Question* (the title of which he will use for his own Norton Lectures) is as follows: "There are three orchestral elements involved: the string ensemble, a solo trumpet, and a woodwind quartet. The strings do indeed play 'pianissimo throughout with no changes in tempo.'" But, says Bernstein, it is more important to notice here that the strings, rather than anything about Druids, "are playing pure *tonal triads*. And against this slow, sustained, purely diatonic background, the trumpet intermittently poses his question—a vague, *non*tonal phrase; and each time it is answered by the wind-group in an equally vague, amorphous way." This pattern of question and answer is repeated more or less the same each time, except the answers grow more ambiguous, more hectic and unnerving, until the final answer emerges as utter nonsense. But, stresses Bernstein, "throughout it all, the strings have maintained

their diatonic serenity, imperturbable; and when the trumpet asks his question for the last time, 'Whither Music?', there is no further answer except for those strings, quietly prolonging their pure G-major triad into eternity." The silences are the objective reality, the tonal background in which the developing dissonance and ambiguities are sounded. All music, Bernstein proposes again, is ultimately and basically tonal, even when it's nontonal. Whether our reaction to *The Unanswered Question* is that of Ives or Bernstein, the metaphysical and musical nature of silence is placed questioningly in front of us. Even if we accept silence as a necessary background for our compositions of sound, problems remain. What still results are significant challenges to the very ways we can conceive of sound and silence, of music and its transformations and ambiguities. Silence and tonality as fundamental metaphysical and musical expressions of our lives open the door to even greater and far-reaching questions.

92. Silence is a statement of the finality of our being. It announces the unities and tensions between death and life, between loss of sound and our linguistic existence. Silence is an inherent component of the fact of language and most clearly and dramatically shows itself in concerns with negation and dissolution. These sentiments are articulated in the music of Mahler. "Ours is the century of death, and Mahler is its musical prophet." The inherent struggle with death is an overwhelming part of Mahler's music and finds a final expression in his Ninth Symphony. This work is illustrative subject matter for a death-ridden understanding of silence and controlled sound. It advances the intriguing ambiguities of how to and why we create in the face of death. Knowing that death is our fate, why do we go on? Why speak to a present and future that is fated to end? This is an old, interminable (repetitive) question, but the uniqueness (variation) of the twentieth and twenty-first centuries' asking it (as Einstein constantly reminded us) is not in our facing death individually but rather being confronted by the problem of surviving global (nuclear) death, total death, and the extinction of the whole race. Mahler, although dying near the beginning of the twentieth-century (1911), was acutely aware of (hypersensitive to) this awful form of existential question yet found in it the ultimate ambiguity of life: human

creativity. In his Ninth Symphony we have a saga of tenderness and terror, of tortured counterpoint and harmonic resignation. We face one repeated farewell after another (to the tonic, to nature, to the world of action, to sound). We are always on the precipice of death. In the fourth and last movement, Adagio, comes the final farewell. It is a presentation of tonality unashamed, but there are no solutions to the struggles that face us. In this last statement of sound, in the last pages of the Ninth Symphony, we reach a sudden coolness, a wide-spaced transparency, a Zen-like immobility of pure meditation, an egoless acceptance of what is; it is sound ending. There are no resolutions, just a quiet dying away into silence, a repeated counting of nothing, of no sounds; this is a loss of the accountable. We lose the sounds we have created, but in their ceasing we find objective sounds still present; "we lose it all but in letting go we have gained everything." That is to say, in the terrifying and paralyzing disintegration of sound that we must ultimately face, and which is constantly going on around us, an important and different possibility of how to live explicitly presents itself, a possibility of accepting finitude.

93. Sensitivities to evil lead to self-reflections on silence. An affirmation that has gone unnoticed in our various concentrations on negation and evil has been exposed in the efforts to count silence. That is, we have been reminded of the ordinary silence that is in plain view. In music, in our creating with controlled and ambiguous sound, we can and we do say "Yes" to a world permeated by evil and death. We create in the face of these negations. Whether our interest is with controlled or natural sound, we are confronted by the question not if we will but "how quickly will we say 'Yes' to the facts of existence?" This is once again a question about voice and audience. Now, however, these concepts are governed by silence. The voice and audience of silence are captured, for instance, in the Mahler Ninth ending. How is it to end? It is not six beats of silence in the midst of controlled sounds, but it is sounds ending with none to follow. When does it end? One conductor raises his hand, spreads five fingers wide, and slowly, one by one, lowers each before a hushed audience. Another sits at rest, makes his baton invisible, and finally closes the score. Yet a different one addresses the audience, after the

first movement, and asks them to help with the magic of the silence of the piece and then (as if on cue) reaches the end as sirens wail outside and come inside as he stands, arms raised, until those sounds end. Another stands motionless holding the moments interminably in his still body and then at last breathes; and the audience—finally—with him. And after it all we (the audience) unleash a Yes!—an applauding, standing affirmation of the silence. Even if we will ultimately lose a sense of what the questions and meanings of our sounds are, we can answer "Yes" to our existence. Ives's and Mahler's musical struggles suggest that one's attitude toward reality can be healthy, loving, or affirming, even given the silent harmony and confirmed desperation that brings dramatic questions about the rationality of living and death. Philosophical questions and conceptual confusions about language and silence can be asked and understood anew through the context of music and its investigation of sound.

94. The fact of language shows the fact of silence. Sharing our feelings and expressions (our music and talk) shows a belief in the importance of silence, for it asks others to listen and attend to the silent harmony of word and world, to the concordance of ourselves and others. But must we not in accepting silence (does not silence) destroy or deny who we are, namely, creatures of language, beings who talk and act? Is not the inarticulate all that is left to us as we contemplate our silent ends? Can we still find something true, meaningful, and creative *to say* in the face of death and silence? Why should we say or do anything at all? The great ambiguity released by these questions is that even in the stark light of total extinction (that terrible negation) humans still create and struggle to find and identify and change themselves. Musical expression, as with other expressions, shows this desire to affirm life and create directly in the growing darkness of nihilism and death. What more positive expression of our common being, of the ordinary, could there be? It is such existential passion and affirmation of ordinary silence that we must not forget or fail to see. We must keep such a reminder before us in whatever we say and do, or do not say and do not do. To be language users, to try to speak and be with others, to create and to make a life with others, is to imply a firm confidence in something, however

transitory that *something* may be. Efforts to mean what we say show a rebellious commitment to creativity and continuing on against all odds, in the face of evil. One might say it shows a weight and worth to the many voices, the ongoing, the temporal and finite, to the repetition and variation of unanswered questions. It shows a struggle to find importance and meaning in our lives without a clear expectation or articulated sense of the possible success of those labors, without a feeling of being assured or firmly justified in what and why we do and say what we do. It shows a virtue of talk and silence.

Silence affirms creation.

95. Silence is all the sounds we don't intend. Several definitions and proposals about the nature of silence have been offered and pursued: silence as consent, as not speaking and letting words go, as moral expression, silence as the rests between sounds, as the background in which sounds occur, as the confrontation with death, negation, and the end of existence. Each of these abstractions is susceptible to understanding silence as a *problem* that needs to be solved (although it is not obviously so in its concrete use for Fanon or Wittgenstein or Gandhi or Mozart or Ives or Mahler). Is there a conception of silence that accepts it as a *fact* in terms of which we must live and create? Our previous definitions have brought some clarity to our investigations but are somewhat restricted and selective; still, another possibility remains to be considered and is found in the music of Cage. Cage's music usually exemplifies particulars and asks questions of existence rather than inform or disrupt or express that (our) existence; and it is often said (probably partly because of this) that his ideas are more important and influential than his music. But can ideas and musical sounds be so separated? Do they lack a common origin or shared forms of expression? If sound is a descriptive and integral element of the ordinary, then we would answer "no" in many contexts where such questions might be asked. Our most recent definitions of silence (i.e., as rests between sounds, the background of tonal soundings, the death that faces us and awaits us) all have contexts of compositional use, but finally these must give way. They are

too narrow for the developing state of affairs in which we now find ourselves or for the descriptions of the ordinary and facts of language that result from reflections on controlled sound. It now is suggested that silence is all the sounds we don't intend. It is that which opens us fully to the world, breaks the barrier between world and ideas, allows that we may no longer usefully know or have a place for the difference between them and necessitates an active rather than a passive existence. Silence leads us out of the world of ideology, away from abstract conceptualizing, and into the whole of concrete life and the possibilities of the ordinary. It is not the opposite of sound but the encompassing of all sound. Silence is all the sounds we don't intentionally make.

96. Quiet deliberation provides opportunities. The music we hear when we are simply quiet provides possibilities of creation. For Cage, the limits and necessities of our world are best treated as facts to be accepted, as occasions for experimentation, as opportunities to attempt new things that have not been tried before. The obstacles and restrictions of our lives should be turned to our advantage rather than accepted as reasons for failure or torment. We must begin to stretch the limits of human expression and experience as Ives and Thoreau, as Stravinsky and Schoenberg, so strongly asked us to do. It is useful, in this regard, to imagine a historical development for our ideas different from what actually occurred. If we do this we see our problems from completely new angles. Cage dispensed with the conflict of tonality and nontonality by working with units of time rather than harmonic or serial progressions. Into these temporal frames he then poured his content and affirmed all sounds. Obstacles are opportunities for new perspectives and ways of seeing and being. When Cage did not have enough space on a dance stage (he actually had too few performers) for any instruments other than a piano, that obstacle allowed him to create the prepared piano. When he was informed (by Schoenberg) that he lacked any harmonic sense, had no feeling for harmony, he changed his approach to music to an investigation not of harmonic relations but of sound itself; sustained duration of sound, where there is less concern with relations and more with being, became his interest. When he found everyone studying intentional sound and felt he could not

improve on those efforts, he decided someone must investigate the nonintentional. Nonintentionality removed the singular, private self and escaped the choices and desires of the individual person. He learned thereby to live with the silences (all the sounds we don't intend) of our world and words. When he found others "following" him in his ways of working, he did something else and left the former concerns to those others. ["I have no students!"] Once, when asked repeatedly (and he declined repeatedly) to give a performance, he acquiesced, finally, and "worked" before the audience on his current textual composition and writing, although carefully amplified and properly timed. Similarly, Thoreau was a great musician, not because he played the flute but because he did not have to go to Boston to hear "the Symphony." He was, says Ives, divinely conscious of the enthusiasm of Nature, the emotion of Her rhythms, and the harmony of Her solitude. He sang of the submission to Nature, the philosophy of contemplation, and the freedom of simplicity—an attitude of reflective patience distinguishing between the complexity of Nature, which teaches freedom, and the complexity of materialism, which teaches slavery. Thoreau's susceptibility to natural sounds, Ives continued, was probably greater than that of many practical musicians. Perhaps the day is coming when music-believers will learn that "silence" is a solvent that gives us leave to be universal rather than personal. Cage, like Thoreau, discovered that natural sounds never cease. Leaving an anechoic chamber, he said he had still heard sounds and was told that that was his body working. "We are always making music" he replied. "What an opportunity."

97. Create so as not to interfere with the sounds continuously going on around us. *4'33"*, a chance-determined composition in three movements, is Cage's most famous and probably most notorious composition. It is four minutes and thirty-three seconds of "silence." Although originally written as a piece for piano, no notes from the keyboard, or from any standard musical instrument, are intentionally played. It is a composition that announces that things should be themselves and relationships between things should be of secondary concern. A few reminders of some of the things said about *4'33"* are helpful. (1) It is his greatest piece (admirers and detractors have said this). "Encore"

(a hope for longer pieces of this kind). (2) It breaks the barrier between world and art and takes us out of the world of abstract creation and into life. The piece is the sounds that naturally happen during the time of the performance; it is those sounds that occur in the concert hall or musical setting (people moving about, coughing and whispering, chairs squeaking and sliding, ventilators humming) and in the outside environment (car horns honking, wind blowing, machines working) that make their way to the audience's ears. It does not allow (or at least diminishes) the threat of dualism and divisions to arise, and thus such efforts and perplexities cannot interfere with the music around us. (3) It exhibits the definition of silence as "all the sounds we don't intentionally make." It is an encompassing of all sound, an equality of all sound. (4) It represents a love and respect for the world (as it is) and asks how quickly we will say "Yes" to our lives as part of (not apart from) the world. With these things being proposed, argued, and often repeated, the significance and moral of *4'33"* might be said to be: We must try to compose and live "so as not to interfere with the music that is continuously going on around us." (Maybe music is ongoing after all and our original definition better and more useful than we last thought.) It is a composition, like much of Cage's music, that allows the ordinary to stand newly and clearly forward and the good it makes possible to be felt and described. We actively listen but do not interfere.

98. Our personal, restricted existence holds the ambiguities and many voices of the world. In his Norton Lectures titled *I-VI: MethodStructureIntentionDisciplineNotationIndeterminacyInterpenetrationImitationDevotionCircumstancesVariableStructureNonunderstandingContingencyInconsistencyPerformance,* Cage expresses an affirmation for our lives. His mesostics, the way he presents the material of his lectures, imitate the world in its manner of operation. The world as a whole is overwhelming, unclear, unprompted. It challenges our cravings for simplicity and understanding. We encounter the mesostics of *I-VI* as we do the world. The whole of the lectures seems unmanageable, but parts are often exciting, enlightening, and discussable. To understand either text or world, we must look to our limited neighborhood, as Thoreau taught us, and to pockets of ideas and develop a sense of self and world

from that local set of particulars. Cage's lectures at Harvard (like Bernstein's) are written to be read aloud. They are to be attentively heard. The sounds of *I-VI* commonly remind us that our hearing has grown rusty and antique in our routine employments and habits of social existence. These newer forms of testament and textual expression celebrate the health and soundness of a Nature we have likely lost. They remind us of the world we lose and forget by so early being weaned to society. The world, like the lectures, is to be listened to with active attention. Look to one's own existence (small neighborhood) and conditions of possibilities for creations and means that develop a sense of and a method to appreciate the overwhelming ambiguities and many voices of the world, and to find an affirmation of life or in other, "older" language, to find the beautiful and good. Listening to the immediate, common world that is before and all around us, to the silence of the ordinary, is the acknowledgment of that greater than ourselves, of words and sounds not our own.

99. The complexity and difficulties of the world leave us with a thirst for sense. The fact of evil leads us to seek meaning in the overwhelming ambiguities and voices of the world. How much can one hope to understand of such multifaceted particulars? What value can there be in confronting the inexhaustible totality of examples? Take a more restricted case. How much does one learn or receive or remember from any specific lecture of reasoned and ordered presentation of words? How much from a poetic or a chance-determined text? How much does one take from Bernstein's lectures or Cage's Norton Lectures? *The Unanswered Question* seeks to be informative but is overwhelmed by confusions and unanswered problems as it reaches its end. *I-VI* is not informative but does have a counterpoint of questions and answers at the bottom of each page that often encourages the reader to continue to try to find meaning in the larger whole. (However, the question of "how much more informative or intelligible is the subtext than the main body of mesostics?" is immediately raised as one begins its reading.) It is worth noting that, in their efforts to discuss world, word, and self, Bernstein emphasizes choice and controlled sound, whereas Cage stresses nonchoice and nonintentional sound. Interestingly, our thirst for

sense and our wish to understand is far greater in *I-VI*. In a certain respect, the lectures of *I-VI* provide a rehearsal for listening to the world. They are restorative and therapeutic. They present us with the greatest confusion that may yet have "the most perfect order as its foundation." They are *rerum concordia discors,* the discordant concord of the world, "a true and complete picture of the nature of the world, which rolls on in the boundless confusion of innumerable forms, and maintains itself by constant destruction." The sounds of *I-VI* cause us to embrace the smallest of familiar repetitions. Their reverberations can be thought of as an attestation that there is perpetually a further possibility of ourselves, for which it is the task of the genuine provocateur to encourage us to find. At the same time, the lectures are a demand for the further possibility of (anarchistic) culture; call it the provision of the means of expression. Our thirst for sense reminds us of opportunities we may have forgotten and opens us to possibilities that we always have before us and that hierarchical society has prevented our properly seeing or hearing or considering.

100. The fact of evil is best faced with our ears. This largely unnoticed possibility and unsaid claim are offered and illuminated in *I-VI*. Although the text is not readily informative, several specific points of argument and contention can be made about the individual six lectures—although each lecture does repeat the material of the others and thereby each comments on each. (Repetition of anything is most extreme when the source material is slight and is less excessive when the complexity of material is great or markedly overwhelming.) (I.) Notice characteristics and aspects of our ways of living that we haven't noticed before. Pockets of ideas carry one through confusions of the whole. Give facts not problems. Provide questions not answers. Creativity lies in asking what has not been asked. Pay attention differently than you have been taught. Self-alteration and recovery are constant possibilities that are before us. Chance operations are means of answering questions other than by intentions. They involve discovery and enjoyment of investigation. Using chance operations affirms our shared existence and denies efforts at competition and privacy. Understand the world in ways we don't intend. (II.) Write music that does not interrupt the silence. What is said about one

way of making music need not necessarily be said about another. There are different ways to love sound and music. (III.) Music as a public and social occasion serves as a metaphor for the type of society we would like. Our current societies are not good or just, but our current lives can be efforts at setting about to be good and just. We can make a life that is meaningful and accountable. (IV.) Allow for and be prepared for the unexpected, unpredicted, and unforeseen. Our performances and lives will be interrupted and our rational plans disrupted. Create with a tolerance of interruptions. (V.) The ordinary and nonspecial is important. Avoid a personal specialness through chance procedures. Chance (not randomness) provides a way of becoming free of our likes and dislikes. The opportunity to pay attention to something that is not routinely offered is what these lectures invite. When others perform works or read texts unlike what we do or had proscribed, that doesn't *ruin* the idea of the work, it just *changes* it. Music that does something rather than says something is of most interest. Difficulty is not the point of music. Most of life is difficult, but it is worth paying attention to its details, and paying attention to the unplanned or the uninteresting is valuable. Seeking the unique insight never reveals a unique self. (VI.) Noises and uncontrolled sound allow one to face and consider the possibilities of anarchism. Tonality insists on hierarchy and classes; anarchy embraces the equality of sound. If you love noises, then you can love the people or the sounds for which the rules of harmony were not made. Beauty in music is often confused with something that lets the ears lie back in an easy chair. Many sounds that we are used to do not bother us, and for that reason we are inclined to call them beautiful. Do not try to get some place as much as try to pay attention in certain ways that we may not have before. It is not getting places, but paying attention, listening attentively, that is important. With these perspectives and turnings declared, it might be said further that the moral of *I-VI* is that the difficulties of life and the facts of the world are (often) best faced (initially) with our ears. Confront evil with an active attention to all the sounds we don't intend.

101. The natural goodness and livability of our lives is exhibited in attention to sound and creation. Schoenberg introduces

a democratization of notes, but autonomy and objectivity remain distant. Cage seeks to give equality to all sounds. He tried to compose and live so as "not to interfere with the music that is continuously going on around us." This is ordinary anarchism, where it is accepted that people can take care of and think for themselves. In Cage's music, instead of hierarchical relations of tones, we are faced with the individual qualities and characteristics of each occasion of sound. Cage explores sounds as individual entities rather than as links in a logical sequence. It might be said that for him metaphysics replaces epistemology; a concern for things used rather than relations of things removes contexts for problems of knowledge, removes our attempting and needing to know. In order to write music as Cage did, to take silence as seriously as he did, you have to assume that people are good and able to take care of and think for themselves. It is an anarchistic way of composing and living. "But it also was a way of life that often caused its proponents to embrace the irrational and nonscientific. Must we do that as well?" As Cage said about Mao, "We don't have to follow him there." As some have said of Berkeley, he was "the first to enunciate it positively, and he has thus rendered an immortal service to philosophy, although the remainder of his doctrines cannot endure." Carefully read the influential, historical thinkers combining a partial yes and a partial no from their writings (as King has taught us), avoiding the trap of accepting uncritically everything written by anyone. Cage's music is a way of life that conveys the natural goodness and livability of our ordinary lives. It expresses how we might live and how he did try to live. When, for instance, his dozens of apartment neighbors were awakened and disturbed for a whole night because a fire alarm malfunctioned and repeatedly sounded, Cage "remained in bed, listened carefully to its pattern and worked it into [his] thoughts and dreams; and slept very well." Listening deliberately and not desperately gives a way to live in the world with assent and healthful creation.

102. Factual limits establish possibilities. If the conditions of controlled sound, as discussed here, are real, one should certainly have the right to dream of them occasionally as a sanctuary and as answering what troubles us. We do so dream from

time to time. Yet two tranquil voices have always kept us from that satisfaction: One has a friend's face, the other a stranger's. "Enough of these passions, its time to awaken and serve reality." "Do you truly believe these things you say?" We do our best to answer these voices and improve our nature not by harm but by means of meaning and consistency. But the price has been high. One sometimes manages to behave morally but never to be moral. Humans sometimes seem to be nothing but a walking injustice—a featherless biped who makes mistakes. To be of passion is to yield to injustice. This is the life of the body and why some have argued for the need to be free of material existence if we are to achieve our moral ends. Surely, we should never claim to be a just person. This has never been our aim or conclusion. We have said only that we should set about to be just—and also that such an ambition involves suffering and unhappiness. But is this distinction so important? It is what we fight for and must preserve. We know (without much effort or reflection) our disorder, the violence of certain instincts, the graceless abandon into which we can throw ourselves. But we also know better now (because of our struggling efforts and reflections) the limits of our talk and action. We know better our possibilities. Often when we thought we were moving forward we were losing ground. Someday, when a balance is established between what we are and what we say and do, perhaps then, and we scarcely dare write it, we shall be able to construct the work of which we dream. "Shrill sound never roused me from my slumbers." Musical creation and expression are efforts that exhibit the silent threaded order of word and world and allow the meaningful possibility of a life that can be called good. Music can quiet and sober desperate lives. One must imagine Cage happy.

103. Living consistently with silence and the experience of sound is a justified response to the fact of evil. Creating music, as it has been suggested we are constantly (nonintentionally) doing, and making an effort to create consistently in terms of the silence of word and world, of the harmony that is the ordinary, is a life that is accountable. There is logic to such a life. Each morning brings the right-minded invitation to embrace repetition and variation, to renew the self again and again, and to make a

life of plainness and innocence equal to that of Nature. This we may now better understand. But it should not go unsaid that we also feel (not just reason and argue) it to be so. We feel this in our bones. Even given the logical arguments, nothing prevents us from fantasizing that we shall succeed where others have failed, from imagining that we shall place at the center of this work of words the admirable silence of our elders and one person's effort to rediscover a justice or a love to match this silence. Music, it may be true, does not deliver us from the evil that is life. It may at best only be able for short, precious moments to offer occasional consolation from the sufferings that surround us. But temporary or occasional respite is still not nothing. The few common, nonintentional sounds we find in ourselves hold our origin and consequences, and from them we must start. We must learn to hear, and this is what music can teach us, the variations that we thought were only repetitions. Maybe, in fact, our musical moments, our musical experiences and understandings, can find extension by our learning to listen anew and to hear more fully the silence and sounds of our lives. We can learn, perhaps, to confront evil with our ears. In the dream that life often is, here is the human, who finds truths and loses them in the struggle and living with finitude, who staggers through wars, tormented cries, the folly of justice and love—in short, through pain— toward that tranquil home where death itself is a happy silence. But now, because of our present efforts, we can offer and give ourselves and others more; argument can replace or stand beside such feelings and dreaming. What we do is to bring words back from their ideological temptations and passions to their everyday, controlled use. A life consistent with ordinary silence is a life justifiably facing evil.

Creating by way of the natural silences is an accountable response to evil and violence.

104. The symphonies of nature know no rests. The world is never quiet; even its silence eternally resounds, in vibrations that often escape our ears. As for those that we perceive, they carry sounds to us, occasionally a note or a chord, never a song. Music exists,

however, in which symphonies are completed, where melody gives its form to sounds that by themselves have none, and where finally a particular arrangement of notes extracts from "natural disorder" a unity that is satisfying to many a mind and heart. We cannot, living and suffering as we do, do without something that is greater than we are. That is not a statement of human need for mystical transcendence but the fact of our life of language, and in it is the desire and power to create, to affirm. No form of expression can survive on total denial alone. Humans can allow themselves to denounce the total injustice of the world and then demand a total justice that they alone will create. But they cannot consistently assert the total disharmony or meaninglessness of the world. Words cannot be prostituted with impunity. To create in terms of the silences of the world, we must simultaneously reject and exalt certain aspects of our existence. Creating as such disputes reality but does not hide from it. This struggle is not something our efforts and philosophy ignores no matter how strongly it insists on our facing the ordinary rather than fleeing from it. The extraordinary is a capacity of and provides access to the ordinary. To be really realistic, an ordinary description would have to be endless. But perhaps there is a living transcendence, of which silence carries the promise, which can make this mortal and limited life and world preferable to and more appealing than any other. Just as there is no nihilism that does not end by supposing a value, so there are no ways of creating in terms of silence that can transcend and reject our ordinary reality. Formalism can succeed in purging itself more and more of real content, but there is always a limit. The ordinary is that limit. The only real formalism would be silence if, that is, silence were not continuously resounding. Quiet never is the world. Its silence reverberates ceaselessly repeating sounds and echoes, in measures that generally we do not hear.

105. The ordinary is repetitive silence. It is the nonintentional, objective, brute particulars of the world. The ordinary is the daily peace of constant, quiet stirring of repetitive life. It is continuous, unplanned, simultaneous, ever-present, ongoing sounds. This is what is partially meant when we speak of the fact or objectivity of language, of repetition and variation. This is what

is meant by ordinary silence. It is the repetition of surrounding sound, the nonintentional conditions of possibility of what we say and do, of what we intend and mean. Ordinary silence is all the sounds we don't intend, the sounds continuously going on around us. Its repetitions can bring boredom—boredom not of emptiness but of prolonged urgency. We investigate deliberately the specific topic of "just plain evil." It is found to be a fact or a problem. It is met with either nonviolence or violence. Violence is confronted with meaningful language. Acting nonviolently is a derived affirmation of the silence of the ordinary. The ordinary is repetition and variation, silence and peace. It is nonintentional sounds; the classic, daily background of life. The ordinary is objective, repetitive talk and action. It is the understated fusions of word and world. We can make our life accountable by creating consistently in terms of the natural silences that endlessly and incessantly present themselves to the attentive ear, by creating in terms of the ordinary. This is where the logic of our arguments and contexts of concern take us.

106. We are contesting a lie and a fact with an affirmation. On the one hand, we are tired of criticism, of disparagement, of spitefulness—of nihilism, in short. It is essential to condemn what must be condemned, but swiftly and firmly. On the other hand, one should praise at length what still deserves to be praised. After all, that is why we are creators, because even the work that negates still affirms something and does homage to the wretched and magnificent life that is ours. This is all to say that we should in our struggles feel solidarity with others, acknowledge the ordinary. Tomorrow the world may burst into fragments. In that threat hanging over our heads there is a lesson of truth. As we face such a future, hierarchies, titles, honors, self-possessions, and glorifications are reduced to what they are in reality: a passing puff of smoke. There is little or no interest in the "passing" world and discussion of its social problems. Evil is a fact (such is the world), and the particular and immediate concerns that try to occupy our attention reemphasize that. "If we read of one man robbed, or murdered, or killed by accident, or one house burned, or one vessel wrecked, or one steamboat blown up, or one cow run over on the Western Railroad, or one mad dog killed, or one lot of

grasshoppers in the winter,—we never need read of another. One is enough." We confront the fact of evil by listening deliberately to the sounds we don't intend and then, if we must, describing particular facts of concern or interest, which will or might allow a proper sense of the possibilities of our lives. Acknowledging evil as a fact opens us to listening to all we don't intend (silence) from which we can regain a familiarity with the depth of the systematic order of our being, with a stability and agreement likely challenged or lost in so facing evil. That, then, allows description of what is (we resist explanation, problem-solving, and remaking and interfering with the world but answer our continual thirst for language) and produces reminders of the conditions of possibility that expose choices of living with, affirmations of, the facts (linguistic phenomenology and conceptual reminders). From evil to music to metaphysics to ethics we wind our way and thereby we turn evil inside-out. We ask: "How to act justly?" And we answer by asking: "How to talk sensibly?" Sometimes only silence is the answer. No just words or just acts seem possible. So the only certainty left to us is that of naked suffering, common to all, intermingling its roots with those of a stubborn hopeless hope. War, disease, and disasters of all and various kinds result in the temptation of hatred. Seeing beloved friends and relatives, even those who are strangers, swept away and killed is not a schooling in generosity. But the pull and enticement of loathing and aversion have to be overcome. This may seem impossible, and maybe we are fighting a lie in the name of a half-truth. But one may even have to fight a lie in the name of a quarter-truth. This is our situation at present: to fight for meaningful distinctions as important as humans themselves.

107. Instead of the judge and the oppressor, the creator. "This will be our response to violence: to make music more intensely, more beautifully, more devotedly than ever before." Every act of creation, by its mere existence, denies the world of master and slave, fights against powerless desperation. The inevitability of nature's wrath and the appalling society of tyrants and slaves, in which we survive and continue to be, will find its transfiguration and death only on the level of creation. Platitudes of dogma and critical or negative reaction and protest are not sufficient or

useful. Affirm, acknowledge, admit, allow, begin, commiserate, conceive, create. Let the social order and its governments, for instance, die their own death, by their own hand, through their inconsistencies and greed. Tyranny is a habit; it has the capacity to develop and does develop into an infectious disease. The best of humans may become coarsened and degraded, by the force of habit, to the level of a savage beast. Blood and power are intoxicants. The possibility of arbitrary power acts like a contagion on the whole of society, and such despotism is a constant temptation. A society that contemplates such manifestations and looks on them indifferently and calmly is already corrupted at its roots. Creation, it is true, is imperiled by the organized spirit of totality and tyranny, but the reverse is true as well. To speak and write reflectively and deliberately, today and maybe always, is to create dangerously. The breaking of habits is seldom easily done or received well. We must find out how, among the police forces of so many ideologies (how many churches), the strange liberty of creation is possible, how significant talk is feasible. The state rejects ordinary silence and thereby meaningful distinctions. It must do so to justify itself. Modern conquerors can kill but do not seem to be able to create. We seem to know at times how to create but cannot justifiably kill. This, then, is our wager: to create rather than to judge. You assert that humans are not good or rational or able to make proper decisions for themselves. You justify this by emphasizing the empirical data of political results and governmental activity of citizens and leaders. You point, for evidence, to a system that mocks all that is good and valuable in humans. And then you conclude that humans are weak, vicious, irrational creatures? Why don't you look at the contexts of volunteers, natural disasters, mutual aid, everyday accidents, or daily, face-to-face life? Is it not possible that humans are not bad or insufficiently good but merely are beings hampered with a plodding, centralized system of bad choices? The strange condition of our time (as Camus has stressed) is that innocence is called on to justify itself—as though we do not know how to talk or know what the word means (I have not learned English). The state presupposes its innocence; and those who loudly and politically defend or speak in the name of those mistreated are speaking, they say, for innocence, for justice. But the strangeness and emptiness of these proclamations can be seen now in the conceptual and logical work on harm and justice, violence and virtue, evil and silence. What is one meaningfully asking in saying that innocence must justify itself? We may no longer need to wonder, in the light of ordinary language philosophy, what the question meaningfully is asking; and we seemingly know how to answer such contemptuousness in our common lives. When innocence is called on to justify itself it replies by creating, by listening to and affirming the ordinary—not by protesting, criticizing, negating existence. Creating rather than judging will be its answer.

108. Deliberate attention to the ordinary settles the fact of evil. Accepting and attending to silence is asking for patience, inviting tolerance and persistence. Learning such patience requires suffering and a willingness to stand for and speak for humankind. It is to try to voice justifiable desires and arguments. *It is never just to harm anyone; create and affirm in terms of ordinary silence.* These are the rules of action for world and word expressed in our philosophy. Of course, stating rules and *then* making them meaningful, utilizing them in the contexts of our lives of language and action, may be extraordinarily—that is, ordinarily—difficult or even impossible. How are we to live? Acknowledge the objectivity of language and follow the reasoning of nonviolence; uphold the agreement of word and world and create in terms of the silences and grammar of our lives. In the face of evil, we are to speak as though each word counts no matter the repetitions and responsibilities. We will deliberately choose to speak rather than not, although our words may be long in coming, with a sense of creating and affirming existence by means of such talk. Such a life is an exercise never finished and a task never accomplished. We may never be able to realize or put to practice our identified rules of action. However, if we are to fail, it is better, in any case, to have stood on the side of those who choose life than on the side of those who are destroying it. (We stand with those provocateurs from Socrates to Cage who test our tolerance of self-reflection, of questions, of interruptions. We stand with those who find little or no causal order to the moral world, and who seemingly get nowhere, but who persistently stay in place because their patient

effort is directed at finding what is important, not at reaching some unreflective end.) The conclusion is simple. It will consist of saying, in the very midst of the sound and fury: "Let us affirm and say 'Yes' to our existence." Perhaps, if we listen attentively, we shall hear, amid the uproar of empires and states, a faint flutter of wings, the gentle stirring of life and hope. Some will say that this hope lies in a nation, others in a noble person. We believe, rather, that it is awakened, revived, nourished by the multitude of "solitary" individuals whose deeds and words every day negate frontiers and the crudest implications of ideology and history. Is it possible continuously to reject injustice without ceasing to acclaim the nature of humans and the good of the world? Our answer is yes, and it is now presumably quite obvious that such a proposal is born of an overwhelming possibility of evil and suffering and a firm decision to face them by means of language.

❖ *Evil is justly faced with an affirmation of the silence of the ordinary. (Create consistently with and by way of the silent harmony of word and world.)*

Supplements to First and Second Books

Supplements to First and Second Books

The temptation is overwhelming to say something further, when everything has already been described. Whence this pressure? What produces it? The difficulty here is: to stop.

Contents

Chapter One
Words Not My Own

(Remarks on foreword, pr–1, 6, 66, 85)

Foreword: "it is still likely the text will be understood best by someone who has already said or read the words that are used in it—or at least similar words."

Many of the words of the First and Second Books are found here:
Socrates: Plato's *Republic, Apology, Crito*
Aristotle: *Metaphysics, Nicomachean Ethics*
Thoreau: *Walden, Civil Disobedience*
Goldman: *The Psychology of Political Violence*
Dostoevsky: *The Brothers Karamazov, The Idiot, Notes from the House of the Dead*
Fanon: *The Wretched of the Earth*
Camus: *The Rebel, Letters to a German Friend, Reflections on the Guillotine*

Schopenhauer: *The World as Will and Representation*
Bernstein: *The Unanswered Question*
Rousseau: *Essay on the Origin of Languages*
Schoenberg: *Style and Idea*
Ives: *Essays Before a Sonata*
Cage: *I–VI*

Many are also found here:
Wittgenstein: *Tractatus Logico-Philosophicus, Philosophical Investigations*
Austin: *Philosophical Papers, How to Do Things with Words*
Cavell: *Must We Mean What We Say?, The Claim of Reason*

Some are still to be found elsewhere:
Beauvoir: *The Second Sex*
Einstein: *Atomic War or Peace*
Emerson: *Essays: First and Second Series*
Gandhi: *Satyagraha*
Kierkegaard: *Either/Or, Concluding Unscientific Postscript*
King: *Pilgrimage to Nonviolence*
O'Neill: *Long Days Journey into Night*
Veblen: *An Inquiry into the Nature of Peace and the Terms of Its Perpetuation*
Anonymous

Preliminary Remark, First Book: "(In fact, it loudly proclaims to be only the words of others—it is best to avoid the beginnings of evil.)"

Removing these words from the parentheses, by a constrained footnoting of some of remark one of the First Book, helps show the structure, the repetition, and the variation of the whole text. (It is also a reminder that silence is an expression of sourcelessness and unassertiveness.)

We talk and act.[1]

1. The world is[2] our word.[3] It wears the colors and expresses the sounds it does by means of the things we say and do.[4] A word has meaning in its use, in the context of a sentence. A sentence has meaning in a language and a language requires a form of life. A form of life has significance only in a world. A world has meaning within the context of a word.[5] There is more to the world, to be sure, than we can talk about, more than we can say about any particular world or aspect of the world[6] ["I can't put it in words, you must experience it for yourself," "what we continue to face and live with is not to be described or explained," "that world is strange and incomprehensible to me"]; but it is empty to suggest the world might be different from what we do or say, as there is no possibility of our having any demonstration or representation of how it might be different from any way in which we might talk about or act in it. "Different from what?" would be the pressing question posed in such a context or elicited by such a claim.[7] It might be objected that facts simply are and we humans try our best to come to terms with them. But this, of course, had to be said, and no matter how hard we try to imagine a world of mere fact, without even the word "fact" with which to think and speak of it, the moment we try to give shape to these inchoate imaginings we must use words. It is seductive to consider a fact-in-itself, but a fact "as such" would be something we could literally say nothing about, must necessarily be silent about.[8]

---

1. Wittgenstein, *Remarks on the Foundations of Mathematics* [321].

2. Schopenhauer, *The World as Will and Representation* [first sentence], and Wittgenstein, *Tractatus* [first sentence].

3. Austin, *Philosophical Papers*, "Performative Utterances" [236].

4. Emerson, *Essays: First and Second Series*, "Experience" [259], and Cavell, *The Senses of Walden*, "Thinking of Emerson" [128].

5. Cavell, *The Senses of Walden* [112].

6. Camus, *The Myth of Sisyphus* [14].

7. Wittgenstein, *Philosophical Investigations* [#227].

8. Van Buren, *The Edges of Language* [58-59], and Wittgenstein, *Tractatus*, [last sentence].

Chapter Two
Extended Contents

(Remarks on First and Second Books)

First Book: Just Plain Evil

We talk and act.

1. The world is our word.
2. Talk and action are materially inseparable.
3. Language and world exist in harmony.
4. There is an unfated connection between meaning and saying.
5. The ordinary is unapproachable.
6. There is a logic to each word we speak.
7. A respect for the ordinary is a necessary beginning.
8. Living deliberately is the task of accepting finitude.

Justifiable action is a question of harm.

9. Individual or collective action may not be just.

10. Justice, good, and virtue are mutually exclusive from harm, evil, and injustice.
11. Injured or harmed humans are worse with respect to human virtue.
12. To do wrong or retaliate with a wrong is never right.
13. Socratic questioning is a nonviolent activity that makes enemies.
14. One who does not know everything cannot justifiably destroy everything.

Harm to innocents is just plain evil.

15. The suffering of others enlivens retribution.
16. Sensitivities to evil lead to violence.
17. Unfeeling indifference and intentional evil produce desperation.
18. It is not individuals but human nature that is at stake.

Evil is met by violence and nonviolence.

19. Evil is eliminated or accepted.
20. Evil challenges the rationality of existence.
21. It is better not to be than to be.
22. Evil is not faced but hidden.
23. Evil, as opposed to what?
24. Evil stands within the harmony of being.
25. The empirical data of evil restricts generalizations.
26. Evil can be demarcated.
27. A categorical assertion and a disputable judgment breathe in the uses of evil.
28. Justified action faces a conflict and choice.
29. Living in the world involves a choice of intolerance or acknowledgment.
30. Equivocations on "evil" threaten clarity of thought.
31. Evil shows how we stand in the world.

54. Privileged authority leads to violence, injustice, and murder.
55. Nihilistic assertions cannot mean what they say.
56. Violence and nonviolence speak in disagreement.
57. Violence is stopped at its source of language destruction.
58. Violence or nonviolence is the choice.
59. Reflective murder and violence are never justified.
60. Speaking is restorative.

It is never just to harm anyone. (Neither to do wrong nor to return a wrong is ever right.)

Second Book: Ordinary Silence

We do and do not talk.

61. The world is silent.
62. Words and silence are materially inseparable.
63. The ordinary background of our life of language is repetition and variation.
64. The fact of evil reduces us to silence.
65. Evil is faced with grammar.

Repetition and variation identify controlled sound.

66. The ordinary is a declaration that words are not our own.
67. The roots of sound and song are found in nature and word.
68. Music is regular vibrations and sound waves that are purposefully varied and systematized.
69. Voice and audience introduce questions about division and unity, self and others.
70. Music is a revelation of the unity of existence.
71. A repetitive principle gives sound its musical qualities.
72. Variation is inseparable from repetition.

Silence affirms creation.

95. Silence is all the sounds we don't intend.
96. Quiet deliberation provides opportunities.
97. Create so as not to interfere with the sounds continuously going on around us.
98. Our personal, restricted existence holds the ambiguities and many voices of the world.
99. The complexity and difficulties of the world leave us with a thirst for sense.
100. The fact of evil is best faced with our ears.
101. The natural goodness and livability of our lives is exhibited in attention to sound and creation.
102. Factual limits establish possibilities.
103. Living consistently with silence and the experience of sound is a justified response to the fact of evil.

Creating by way of the natural silences is an accountable response to evil and violence.

104. The symphonies of nature know no rests.
105. The ordinary is repetitive silence.
106. We are contesting a lie and a fact with an affirmation.
107. Instead of the judge and the oppressor, the creator.
108. Deliberate attention to the ordinary settles the fact of evil.

Evil is justly faced with an affirmation of the silence of the ordinary. (Create consistently with and by way of the silent harmony of word and world.)

Further Expansion of Contents

100. The fact of evil is best faced with our ears.
      I. Understand the world in ways we don't intend.
      II. There are different ways to love sound and music.

Chapter Three
Dark Matters

(Remarks on 1–3, 61, 63, 87)

The imagination and insight of those providing the contemporary likely story of the universe and its origins are something truly marvelous. As with past efforts, current presentations stress that fundamental forces are at work in the world. Whether we talk of gravity, electromagnetism, the strong and weak nuclear forces, or earth, air, fire, and water, basic organizing components are asserted and found to dominate the cosmos. Today, as often was contemplated before, these forces are themselves thought likely to be but different manifestations of a single unified influence. That cohesive actuality that was and controlled the universe in its earliest, hottest moments ultimately unfolded or divided and split apart from itself as the universe cooled. Strings, or minute vibrating loops, became more diverse and prominent; these were not masses and forces as we have standardly understood them but rather the one-dimensional, Planck-sized (10^{-33} centimeters) elements out of which those larger effects and physical features were to come to be. Originally, then, the cosmos was inconceivably small and its energy density was indefinitely great. At its earliest beginning the universe was radically different from the vastness and sparseness that we now observe, as it was unimaginably minuscule and dense.

In so talking about our universe we must expect that much is hidden from us and that surprising conclusions often will result, for the universe is imposing, and we are creatures of limited experience and intelligence. There could be, for all we will ever know, an indefinite number of possible universes, or uncountable aspects and layers to our universe. The world we see is just a tiny bit of a much greater universe forever out of our view. We do now seem to know that the physical matter needed to account for the order of the universe must be much greater than that for which we have accounted. Galaxies would have disintegrated long ago if they were not held together by more gravity than our standard and past accounts of matter have allowed. Without substantial dark matter—the subatomic particles left after the initial beginnings of the universe—the galaxies of celestial material could not rotate as fast as they do and would fly apart rather than hold their forms. Things could not be as they are unless they were being reigned in by dark matter. If all the luminous substance in the cosmos—the planets, gas clouds, stars, and galaxies—were smoothed out and spread uniformly throughout the universe, the result would be a virtual vacuum everywhere. This means that the majority of matter of the universe is not what we commonly experience but is primarily mysterious elementary particles that do not interact with light. So the clusters of matter we experience are not made up of the same stuff as most of the universe, which is for the most part an invisible form of energy—dark energy—that fills all space and has the property of making space expand, has the property of repulsion, or antigravity. The universe, therefore, is not principally the collected matter that has always caught our eyes; to our surprise, it is instead the dark matter, or expanding space that is opening between the clusters of galaxies.

However the likely story is presented, any description of the conditions of such possibilities must enlighten or inform such talk. We continue to be freed from the earth-centered and human-centered universes. We know that humans are just a small excess of the condensed matter of the cosmos, a strange interlude between different orderings of matter, an insignificant phenomenon, and that the universe is something largely different from us. The earth itself and its human inhabitants may even be quite unusual. In almost all other parts of existence, the radiation levels are too high, the right chemical elements too rare in abundance, the hospitable planets too few in number, and the rain of killer space rocks too intense for life ever to evolve into something relatively advanced. But maybe the numbers and possibilities are much greater than supposed. Perhaps our universe, although rare in an overall sense, is still just one among countless many, so that universes with differing amounts of dark energy might be more common than we thought, and life of our sort more likely than sometimes believed or calculated. But then again, most of these possible universes would expand too rapidly to form stars, planets, or life. Still, universes with smaller values of expansion might be very rare—yet more abundant than we have allowed.

Whatever the calculations of these possibilities, our universe and any compatible others with "advanced" life must have an optimal value for that human or evolved life to be. It is not a fortunate or lucky coincidence that thinking beings and current cosmic acceleration exist at the same time and in harmony. Or maybe we will find evidence to persuade us differently about chance happenings in the universe. The thinking and evidence about the formation and development of the universe, as was the case with considerations about fire and air, swings first one way and then another. The range of possibilities is seemingly endless and has the potential to lessen or strengthen our insistence on the one and only explanation of all that is. But no matter what the successes and frustrations, we can at least say this: Because a life of words and action exists in at least one place in the universe (however rare and fleeting), because we talk and act, the proposed physical laws governing the universe, the fundamental forces and particles—whether they be points or vibrating strings—have to be such that they acknowledge this fact of language, these forms of life. The theories of the actualities, vibrating strings, elemental particles, and physical laws governing the universe must be such that they allow for talk and action, allow for the conditions that make possible the particular talk and action of concern in physical investigations, for the talk of fundamental forces, hidden energy, and unpredictable, surprising results. Without such there would be no "dark matter." This is just to say: Our entire explanatory practice is stored within our language. Such an ordinary reminder and description of fact must not be forgotten or conflict with whatever instructive and universe-revealing efforts are offered. Investigations of the "hidden" must not stop short of the ordinary conditions that make them possible and that unceasingly push us to our limits.

Objectivity of Language

Language is rule-governed.
To be rule-governed, there must be criteria of correctness.
A private language has no criteria of correctness.
There is no private language.

Remarks on 198–384 of Wittgenstein's Philosophical Investigations

0. Can there be a private language?
1. A private language would be an unteachable language. It would be useable and understandable by a single individual and only that individual. 243, 256
2. Language is rule-governed because it is rules that set limits and provide possibilities for such things as meaning, descriptions, and understanding. 240, 384
3. Rules are obeyed or followed in accord with a specific interpretation or practice, which in turn depends on specific human agreements in judgment and action. 206, 198, 199, 241, 242
4. To follow or obey a rule there must be criteria of correctness and identity. 258

5. Nothing can be a criterion of correctness or identity unless it can show that a mistake has been made or that a difference is possible. 227

6. The only possible criterion of correctness or identity for a private language is a subjective justification. Appeals to memory would be the prime possibility for such a subjective justification. 342, 344

7. Subjective justifications such as memory or simply thinking that something is the case cannot by themselves show that a mistake has been made. 265, 202

8. Therefore, there cannot be a private language.

9. If there can be no private language is there then no private experience? Don't I know from my own case alone what pain is or what thinking is? 246, 272

10. Pain and thinking can be all we *say* they are without being subjective, private *objects*, and without our *knowing* them in some private sense. 293, 296

11. The treatment of sensations and mental phenomena as private objects is a misleading picture. 304, 305, 306, 307

12. If inner sensations were private objects, then the person who has the sensations would be able to refer to them, understand them, and know them privately, in a way no one else could. 256, 293

13. It is not possible to refer to, understand, or know our sensations and mental experience in a private way because this would require a private language, not just a private naming. (Naming requires the practice and stage-setting of language to be possible.) 257, 269, 378

14. Therefore, there are no private objects. The picture of sensations as private objects is misleading and produces misuse of words such as "object," "see," "possess," "right." 316, 281, 258

15. Object and thought depend on language use for their particular kind of existence. Grammar tells what kind of object anything is. 290, 294, 373, 371, 372, 251, 252, 247

Chapter Four
Reading the Dictionary

(Remarks on 50, 75)

It has been said that a characteristic of wisdom is not to do desperate things. Reading the dictionary from cover to cover is a deliberate walk of life. Quite a concise dictionary will do, but the use must be *thorough*—patient, calm note-taking is required. The *Concise Oxford English Dictionary* is a suitable choice. Immediately, the discovery of how little we know is put before us and reinforced; how few of the many words that exist we ourselves possess. We find again how wondrous is the inherited experience and acumen of many generations of humans. (This is a slight counterbalance to the plaguing sensitivity that nothing human matters very much; that *our* span of time in the greater cosmos is so insignificant and fleeting that it is hardly worth praise or continuance or attention.)

In such a life, Austin found that the study of excuses was improved by looking at "clumsiness," "absence of mind," "inconsiderateness," and "spontaneous." Similarly, he argued that concern with the beautiful benefited from examination of "dainty" and "dumpy"; that questions about reality must not ignore "illusions," "phony," "directly," and "delusions." These additional terms are a part of a compilation of dictionary data. Two methods suggest themselves in the collection of such linguistic and phenomenological material. Both can be a bit tedious but repaying. One is to read the book through, listing all the words that seem relevant to the task at hand. The other is to start with a widish selection of obviously relevant terms and to consult the dictionary under each. The first is preferable and least prejudicial. The data, it is true, can be extensive (when in doubt, include a term) and slow to assemble (it can take many months or years of one's time); here, for instance, is a partial list of some of the data for about half of the dozen or so words guiding the cover-to-cover work of *Evil and Silence* (although the reflections and data collection started more than a year before the conception and writing of the text).

A–C entries for "ordinary," "evil," "silence," "say" (mean), "harmony," and "first."

Ordinary

acceptable, accustomed, all right, apt, average, banal, banausic, basic, blank, boring, classic, common, commonplace, communal, condition, conventional, customary, criterion, crude

Evil

abhorrent, abominable, absence, abysmal, accursed, ache, adversity, affliction, affront, aghast, agony, alas, amoral, amulet, annus horribilis, antipathy, antithetical, apotropaic, Armageddon, atrabilious, atrocious, avert, awful, bad, badhairday, bale, baleful, bane, barbaric, barbarism, base, beast, bewail, bilious, black, bleak, bogey, burden, calamity, callous, cancer, catastrophic, corrupt, -cide, criminal, cruel

Silence

allay, anechoic, aphasia, aphonia, apoplexy, aposiopesis, breath (under one's), calm, check, composure, curb, curtail

Say (Mean)

address, argle-bargle, articulate, babble, babel, bafflegab, balderdash, bend someone's ear, blather, breath (waste one's), button it, chat, clichéd, communicate, confab, confer, confide, cry, convince, count, counterclaim

Harmony

accordance, agreement, balance, blending, butterfly effect, chime with, commensurable, commonality, compatible, complementarity, concert, concord, concurrent, congruent, consensus, consistent, consilience, consonance, contiguous, continuity, coordinate, correlation, correspond

First

A, abecedarian, aboriginal, aborigine, ahead, alpha, archetype, atavistic, at the outset, base, basic, basis, bedrock, before, begin, birth, bismillah, cardinal, chief, commence, crucial, cosmogenesis, cosmology

Reading the dictionary from cover to cover is a part of the exercise in agreeing about how to reach agreement. It is an effort to understand what *we* say and do, or do not say and do not do; an effort to understand *our* philosophy, as Wittgenstein (the sometimes forgotten author of a spelling dictionary) calls it. It is *in* the linguistic data and the conditions that make it possible that we can (at least in part) find ourselves. That is where *we* are. Reflective and unwearied dictionary reading (searching for *us*) is an activity and exertion that need not be, and likely is not, guided by an end or beacon or a knowing what will be (if anything) accomplished. One sets about the task without knowing exactly what is being done or will be done. Perhaps it will seem that we have too many lives to live to spare so much time for this one. Maybe it is properly judged as madness to undertake such a large task with no sense of clear purpose or end before one. It is true that it is not worth the while to go around the world to count the cats of Zanzibar (go so far for so little return). Yet do this even till you can do better, and you may perhaps find some means to get at last at what is important and interesting and of value. (Dostoevsky tells us how a favorite occupation of many of his fellow convicts was counting the palisades that made the prison fence. Each post slowly became uniquely known by its position and characteristics. Each one meant a day but showed the state of a life. Hopelessness was calmed by such activity. By coming to the end of a row, one could even be genuinely happy.) In this way, reading "cover to cover" comes to mean not a fixed goal of achievement but an exercise to read one page and then possibly the next, to read one word ("consistent to consistent") and then possibly the next. Each step on each page is its own end and purpose, its own entry to a life that counts.

Chapter Five
Pro and Contra

(Remarks on 58)

One instance of the unsettled "I do both" of *The Brothers Karamazov* comes in Part II, Books V and VI. Ivan's carefully ordered (often cited) argument is countered, point for point, in the wandering (often neglected) presentation of the life of Father Zosima. Placing some of the textual quotations side by side makes this more apparent.

"Pro and Contra" and "The Russian Monk"

Rebellion	*The Russian Monk*
1. "I never could understand how it's possible to love one's neighbors.... If we're to come	1. "... do not be afraid of men's sin, love man also in his sin, for this likeness of God's love

to love a man, the man himself should stay hidden, because as soon as he shows his face love vanishes." "It's still possible to love one's neighbor abstractly, and even occasionally from a distance, but hardly ever up close." 236–237

2. "... let us dwell only on the suffering of children ... one can love children even up close, even dirty or homely children.... If they, too, suffer terribly on earth, it is, of course, for their fathers; they are punished for their fathers.... It is impossible that a blameless one should suffer for another, and such a blameless one!" 237–238

3. "I think that if the devil does not exist, and man has therefore created him, he has created him in his own image and likeness." 239

4. "You see, once again I positively maintain that this peculiar quality exists in much of mankind—this love of torturing children, but only children. These same torturers look upon all other examples of humankind even mildly and benevolently, being educated and humane Europeans,

is the height of love on earth. Love all of God's creation, both the whole of it and every grain of sand. Love every leaf, every ray of God's light.... And you will come at last to love the whole world with an entire, universal love." 318–319

2. "Love children especially, for they, too, are sinless.... Woe to him who offends a child." "The people are festering with drink and cannot leave off. And what cruelty towards their families, their wives, even their children, all from drunkenness!" 319, 315

3. "Indeed, how did I deserve that another man, just like me, the image and likeness of God, should serve me?" 298

4. "If the wickedness of people arouses indignation and insurmountable grief in you, to the point that you desire to revenge yourself upon the wicked, fear that feeling most of all; go at once and seek torments for yourself, as if you yourself were guilty of their wickedness. Take those torments upon

but they have a great love of torturing children, they even love children in that sense. It is precisely the defenselessness of these creatures that tempts the torturers...." "Well ... what to do with him? Shoot him? Shoot him for our moral satisfaction?" 241, 243

5. "Oh, with my pathetic, earthly, Euclidean mind, I know only that there is suffering, that none are to blame, that all things follow simply and directly one from another.... Of course I know that, and of course I cannot consent to live by it! What do I care that none are to blame and that I know it—I need retribution, otherwise I will destroy myself. And retribution not somewhere and sometime in infinity, but here and now, on earth, so that I see it myself." 244

yourself and suffer them...." "One may stand perplexed before some thought, especially seeing men's sin, asking one-self: 'Shall I take it by force, or by humble love?' Always resolve to take it by humble love." 321, 319

5. "And ... as for each man being guilty before all and for all, besides his own sins, your reasoning about that is quite correct..." "'What is hell?' And I answer thus: 'The suffering of being no longer able to love.' ... I am and I love." "Oh, there are those who remain proud and fierce even in hell, in spite of their certain knowledge and contemplation of irrefutable truth.... For them hell is vol-untary and insatiable; they are sufferers by their own will." 303, 322, 323

Grand Inquisitor

6. "'Better that you enslave us, but feed us.' They will finally understand that freedom and earthly bread in plenty for everyone are inconceivable together, for never, never will they be able to share among themselves. They will also be

6. "Only a little, a tiny seed is needed: let him cast it into the soul of the simple man, and it will not die, it will live in his soul all his life.... Whoever does not believe in God will not believe in the people of God." "... All my life I have

convinced that they are forever incapable of being free, because they are feeble, depraved, nonentities and rebels." 253

been struck by the true and gracious dignity in our great people, I have seen it, I can testify to it myself." 294, 315

7. "And then we shall finish building their tower, for only he who feeds them will finish it, and only we shall feed them, in your name, for we shall lie that it is in your name.... We shall say that we are obedient to you and rule in your name.... This deceit will constitute our suffering, for we shall have to lie." 253

7. "Everywhere now the human mind has begun laughably not to understand that a man's true security lies not in his own solitary effort, but in the general wholeness of humanity." "'But how can you understand it ... if the whole world has long since gone off on a different path, and if we consider what is a veritable lie to be the truth, and demand the same lie from others?'" 303–304, 300–301

8. "There is no more ceaseless or tormenting care for man, as long as he remains free, than to find someone to bow down to as soon as possible.... Give man bread and he will bow down to you, for there is nothing more indisputable than bread. But if at the same time someone else takes over his conscience—oh, then he will even throw down your bread and follow him who has seduced his conscience.... There is nothing more seductive for man than the freedom of his conscience, but there is nothing more tormenting either." 254

8. "Taking freedom to mean the increase and prompt satisfaction of needs, they distort their own nature, for they generate many meaningless and foolish desires, habits, and the most absurd fancies in themselves. They live only for mutual envy, for pleasure-seeking and self-display.... I ask you: is such a man free? ... Which of the two is more capable of upholding and serving a great idea—the isolated rich man or one who is liberated from the tyranny of things and habits?" 313–314

9. "There are three powers, only three powers on earth, capable of conquering and holding captive forever the conscience of these feeble rebels, for their own happiness—these powers are miracle, mystery, and authority." "We corrected your deed and based it on *miracle, mystery,* and *authority*." 255, 257

9. "Much on earth is concealed from us, but in place of it we have been granted a secret, mysterious sense of our living bond with the other world, with the higher heavenly world, and the roots of our thoughts and feelings are not here but in other worlds.... If this sense is weakened or destroyed in you, that which has grown up in you dies. Then you become indifferent to life, and even come to hate it." 320

10. "And mankind rejoiced that they were once more led like sheep, and that at last such a terrible gift, which had brought them so much suffering, had been taken from their hearts." "Receiving bread from us, they will see clearly, of course, that we take from them the bread they have procured with their own hands, in order to distribute it among them, without any miracle; they will see that we have not turned stones into bread; but, indeed, more than over the bread itself, they will rejoice over taking it from our hands!"... Then we shall give them quiet, humble happiness, the happiness of feeble creatures, such as they were created." 257, 258–259

10. "Look at the worldly and at the whole world that exalts itself above the people of God: are the image of God and his truth not distorted in it? They have science, and in science only that which is subject to the senses. But the spiritual world, the higher half of man's being, is altogether rejected, banished with a sort of triumph, even with hatred." "There is only one salvation for you: take yourself up, and make yourself responsible for all the sins of men. For indeed it is so, my friend, and the moment you make yourself sincerely responsible for everything and everyone, you will see at once that it is really so, that it is you who are guilty on behalf of all and for all." 313, 320

11. "His silence weighed on him. He had seen how the captive listened to him all the while intently and calmly, looking him straight in the eye, and apparently not wishing to contradict anything. The old man would have liked him to say something, even something bitter, terrible. But suddenly he approaches the old man in silence and gently kisses him on his bloodless, ninety-year-old lips. That is the whole answer. The old man shudders.... The kiss burns in his heart, but the old man holds to his former idea." 262

11. "And what is the word of Christ without an example?" "Then the sign of the Son of Man will appear in the heavens.... But until then we must keep hold of the banner, and every once in a while, if only individually, a man must suddenly set an example...." "And if, having received your kiss, he goes away unmoved and laughing at you, do not be tempted by that either: it means that his time has not yet come, but it will come in due course; and if it does not come, no matter: if not he, then another will know, and suffer, and judge, and accuse himself, and the truth will be made full." 294, 304, 321

12. "You mean 'everything is permitted'? Everything is permitted, is that right, is it?" ... "Yes, perhaps 'everything is permitted.'..." 263

12. "And in their own terms, that is correct: for if you have no God, what crime is there to speak of?" 315

(Page numbers are keyed to the Pevear and Volokhonsky translation of 1990.)

Chapter Six
Musical Illustrations

A. References

The following three musical examples, Beethoven's Symphony 6, Mozart's Symphony 40, and Ives's *The Unanswered Question,* are pages from Bernstein's own scores. They illustrate numbers 71, 74, and 91 respectively. [Reference: http://www.leonardbernstein. com/norton_scores.htm]

The first page of Wagner's *Tristan und Isolde* and the first page of *Parsifal* supply details to numbers 80 and 81. [Reference: http://www.dlib.indiana.edu/variations/scores/bfk2835/index .html; http://www.dlib.indiana.edu/variations/scores/baj5813/ index.html] An early page of Debussy's *The Prelude to the Afternoon of a Faun* does the same for number 90. [Reference: http://www .dlib.indiana.edu/variations/scores/bgn9673/index.html]

An original manuscript page from Schoenberg's Opus 23, *Five Piano Pieces* [Reference: http://www.schoenberg.at/scans/ Ms23/Ms23/10.jpg], and the central tone-row from Berg's *Violin Concerto* (section B) and last page of *Wozzeck* [Reference: http:// solomonsmusic.net/wozzeck.htm] are given, clarifying 81 and 83.

The last page of Mahler's Symphony 9 provides further reflection on 92 and 93. [Reference: http://imslp.info/files/ imglnks/usimg/5/5d/IMSLP21194-PMLP48640-Symphony_ No._9_-_IV.pdf], and the first page of Stravinsky's *Petrushka* illustrates 85 [Reference: http://www.dlib.indiana.edu/variations/ scores/aad9501/index.html]; while a passage from Bernstein's Mass and a page of Tchaikovsky's Symphony 6 (again from Bernstein's personal scores) correspondingly exemplify numbers 86 and 87. [References: http://www.leonardbernstein.com/mass_scores .htm; http://www.leonardbernstein.com/norton_scores.htm]

The *4'33"* manuscript page and precursor materials augment 97 [Reference: http://solomonsmusic.net/4min33se.htm], and the mesostics examples from *I–VI* (section E) illustrate 98.

B. Berg's *Violin Concerto* and *Wozzeck*

(Remarks on 83)

Berg's concerto for violin (his last completed work), like a number of his other compositions (*Piano Sonata*, op. 1, *Three Orchestral Pieces*, *Wozzeck, Lulu*), unites a diversity of material. It presents structures of serialism, following the techniques of Schoenberg, with material written in more traditional and tonal forms. Although parts of the score are atonal, as is relatively standard and a general expectation in twelve-tone works, other sections can be said to be in a particular key, and instances and quotations of purely tonal music are present and identifiable, generally forbidden results of the rules of traditional twelve-tone pieces. The concerto's principal tone row reflects this integration and conflict of atonality and tonality:

As with many traditional tone rows, this instance contains all twelve notes of the chromatic scale. However, it is not without tonal nuances. For instance, the first three notes of the row make up a G minor triad, notes three to five are a D major triad, notes five to seven are an A minor triad, notes seven to nine are an E major triad, and the last four notes coupled with the first provide part of a whole tone scale. Berg will also use tonal and programmatic material not directly based on this tone row in parts of the concerto.

Berg used diverse forms of musical expression as a way to connect one kind of music and musician to another and one time to another. His recombinant style of writing was homage to the music of his predecessors and expresses a respect for those composers who meant so much to him. Many a composer does something like that, but not always with the success and innovation found in Berg, or with the depth of reflection on repetition, variation, and silence that such contrasting structures and content brought to many of his compositions. Consider, for instance, the final interlude of *Wozzeck,* which is so powerfully and disturbingly touching for many who hear it. The strength of his compositional presentation in the final sections of the opera is (like the *Violin Concerto*) partly due to an explicit use of tonality in the midst of serialism, due to the way we suddenly at the end of the piece hear harmonically where we are in this atonal "darkness" of sound. Berg "saved" this pure tonal idea and contrast of sound for this last interlude, as he would do similarly many times in other pieces. But here, at the conclusion of his first opera, this use of a variety of musical language was not just musically formal in nature but was directly and concretely able to express the way he felt the subject matter was to be engaged and heard. From that D minor interlude emerges the last scene in the opera where the kids are playing and there's Marie's little boy, who doesn't know that his parents are dead; the music powerfully voices this particular context of life and death. The young boy is blissfully playing on a hobby horse. His last words, and those of the opera, are "hop hop," "hop hop," "hop hop." But the music accompanying this repetition of familiar, childish, innocent sound does not itself end in a common or obviously recognizable way, as Wagner or

Mozart might have done. It doesn't, that is, so much end as, we might say, the composition simply runs out of paper or sound, or it is as though someone closes a door and goes on their way. The boy noticing that he is alone hesitates and leaves. The curtain then falls on the empty stage. But with the curtain closed the music continues. It goes on in repetitive sound and silence. But it is not the tonal sounds and silences we might expect or have heard quite the same way before. The sound repeats and repeats and then simply stops. There is no more. [Reference: http://solomonsmusic.net/wozzeck.htm]

Although quite clearly written, this end is (maybe surprisingly) difficult to perform correctly. The effect should not be that the last note hangs over or lingers on. And the effect should not be that it stops abruptly or hurriedly or expectedly. There are just the repeating notes, and then the last ones, until there isn't another one. The sound is not dramatically sustained or suddenly completed. It just alternates, repeats, and then it stops. Fait accompli. Ende der Oper.

C. Neoclassicism and Variations on an Original Theme

(Remarks on 86, 87)

Taking a specific work as a standard, and using it as a form to be filled with a new content that may or may not intentionally recall the older work (neoclassicism), is a method of Western musical practice found in many traditional twentieth-century composers (e.g., Brahms or Shostakovich). Even someone as revolutionary as Schoenberg found value and necessity in such uses of the forms of the past. This is especially the case with his work of the late 1920s (viz., the *Wind Quintet*, opus 26, the opus 29 *Suite*, and the *Variations for Orchestra*, opus 31). The most determined and fully accomplished of these efforts is probably his *String Quartet no. 3*, opus 30, which is modeled on the famous *String Quartet in A minor* of Schubert.

Early-twentieth-century neoclassicism is found powerfully displayed in such Stravinsky masterworks as *L'Histoire du Soldat* (1918), *Les Noces* (1923), *Oedipus Rex* (1927), and *Symphony in*

Three Movements (1946). They provide, in fact, a benchmark for how the word "neoclassicism" is used in contemporary music.

Just as significantly and maybe more perspicuously, neoclassicism is found in Bernstein's less revered and understudied *Mass: A Theatre Piece for Singers, Players, and Dancers* (1971). Throughout the more than two-hour composition, the traditional form of a catholic Mass is joined with modern content. Bernstein, for instance, filled the "Credo" section of the customary mass form with, among other dissimilarities and tensions, a rock 'n' roll content. [Reference: http://www.leonardbernstein.com/mass_scores.htm]

Such efforts and experiments in objective expressivity are to be found as well in much of the rest of Bernstein's life. The significant influences and the interpretive risks, for instance, of Bernstein's conducting performances (throughout his long career) are hardly to be denied. His post–Norton Lectures performances, in particular, set Bernstein apart from other conductors of the time and from his own previous efforts. These were performances to which it was hard to remain indifferent and on which negative and questioning remarks standardly fell. Although many theoreticians and practitioners at the time were moving toward and championing a reconstructed historical accuracy ("authenticity"), with ever tighter technical and emotional control and pinpoint-precise execution, Bernstein walked forthrightly into a full-blown, total embrace of passionate expression. He luxuriated in sonic sensuousness, as though seeking release from the "normal" performance traditions of the pieces he conducted in order to pursue new revelations in sound. He sought to induce and express personal affirmation and identification with old forms. Bernstein's conducting interpretations in his last two decades of work were cultivating a heightened perception of orchestral sound, importantly including an attention to the interaction of personal voices and objective conventions. His breathtakingly contrasting tempos and unusually measured pacing, often markedly departing from the normal range of tempo-variations encountered in the performing tradition, exemplified this most clearly.

At the core of these performances was an effort at expressive clarity. But it was not always seen or understood as such.

Instead it was often judged as an effort at what some (of the more generous critics) called "purposefully expressive distortion" or "excessive, indulgent mannerisms." These latter comments, however, were unhelpful and unstudied responses at best, even granting the limited contexts in which they were written or said. It was, importantly and more properly, the Stravinskian "objective expressivity" of the Norton Lectures, the sound and grammar of our lives, of voice and audience, that he sought and offered us in his conducting work.

Among the most astonishing of these presentations were, as expected, his Mahler performances. The controlled-self seeking excessive, emotional variations in past repetitions was at home in Mahler's music. But just as exemplary of objective expressivity, but somewhat less expected, were his new performances of such seemingly well-worn works as Haydn, Tchaikovsky, and Sibelius symphonies, and of what was to be the most notorious (and heavily criticized) example of all, Elgar's *Variations on an Original Theme*, the "Enigma Variations." (Recordings that partly preserve these events were made, and even in that context we feel we are not to recreate and listen impersonally, in the name of some dispassionate authenticity, to what Elgar or Haydn—how many symphonies did he write?—or Sibelius "really intended.") We are placed with these performances in the midst of what Bernstein perceived as the music's rich ambiguities (its enigmas) and reverberating immensity of voices. Such concepts played a crucial role throughout the Norton Lectures, and they dominated his later conducting performances.

A direct and simple instance of this reflective and consistent aspect of Bernstein's conducting life can be seen from a page of his personal score of Tchaikovsky's Symphony No. 6 (the *Pathetique*). [Reference: http://www.leonardbernstein.com/norton_scores.htm] On the first page of the second movement, Bernstein wrote: "Simultaneously 2/3—3/2 = ambiguity = charm." He is referring to the unusual 5/4 meter that creates an off-kilter waltz, vacillating between divisions of 3 + 2 and 2 + 3, an example of musical ambiguity and many voices, an instance of that which governed, especially in his last years, his conducting efforts to speak personally to others.

D. *4'33"*

(Remarks on 97)

The idea and inspiration for *4'33"* can be seen in the "White Paintings" of Rauschenberg (especially when they are placed side-by-side). [Reference: http://solomonsmusic.net/4min33se. htm] Cage, in fact, asserted that he was greatly influenced by these panels of white of Rauschenberg ["they gave me the courage I needed to make my conception real"]. The origins of *4'33"*, of course, are not quite that simple, and it is helpful to take notice of a few other facts and sources, as well as silent musical pieces and excursions that preceded and followed the composition of *4'33"*, in order to appreciate to some extent its place in music history.

In his "A Composer's Confessions" of 1948, Cage writes that he has two rather "absurd" desires for new compositions. One was a piece for "12 radios." This would in 1951 become *Imaginary Landscape No.4* and be followed in 1955 by *Speech (for radios and speaker)*. Numerous pieces involving radios would be created by Cage, including his first such effort, *Credo in Us* (1942), and his last, a new adaptation of the 1955 piece, *Speech (for radios and speaker, B-Version)* (1990). The other "absurd" idea was "a piece of uninterrupted silence" to be "4 ½ minutes long" and to be titled "Silent Prayer." This would four years later become *4'33"*.

The timings and length of movements of *4'33"* have some controversy about them. Different texts list different timings. The original Woodstock (first performance) manuscript material is said to give these times: I. 30", II. 2'23", III. 1'40". Several later editions follow this and give the same time markings to the three sections. But other editions from 1960 and 1986, generally following Cage's revisions of the piece, give these measured divisions: I. 33", II. 2'40", III. 1'20". Most performers have used the first set of timings. This seems to make some sense because Cage's revisions were given, in point of fact, to free the piece of its structure and confinements. "We don't have to think in terms of movements any more," he said. He wanted to create a wholly different work from the original and not simply change or improve on it. He would do this specifically with such pieces as *0'00"* (sometimes called *4'33" No. 2*), composed in 1962.

Several musical compositions using silence in an extensive manner preceded Cage's work and publication of *4'33"*. An interesting instance is Alphonse Allais's "Funeral March" for the last rites of a deaf man (1897). This composition consists of twenty-four measures of an entirely blank music manuscript, except for a tempo mark of "Lento rigolando" (rigidly slow). [Reference: http://solomonsmusic.net/4min33se.htm]

Although quite a bit shorter, and not divided into separate movements, this "silent piece" might be judged as basically similar in thought and corresponding rather amazingly to the conception (many have) of *4'33"*. How original and radical, then, was Cage's idea and composition? There is certainly no denying that on first approach the two pieces seem cut from the same cloth and apparently seek similar provocations of feeling and thought. (*Marche Funebre*'s lack of separated movements might, indeed, even be seen as Allais's anticipating Cage's later revisions and thoughts about silence and form.) In his short, prefatory notes to the piece, Allais states that his composition is to be concerned entirely with measurements rather than with sounds.

Although quite enticing in itself and for its time, the similarities of this funeral march to *4'33"* remain, however, relatively fleeting, as do other instances of "silent composition" that are part of the Western canon before Cage's effort. Allais's composition was largely intended to be a joke and had none of the depth and struggle of thinking and presentation that is part of *4'33"*. Cage, as we know, was very serious about *4'33"* and was careful to stress that it was not a gag or act of wit and was not to be presented as such in performance. It is fair to say, in fact, that any list of Cage's principal works would include with all seriousness *4'33"*. (A list I gave in print in 1996 of his most important compositions consisted of: *Credo in Us* [1942], *Sonatas and Interludes* [1948], *Williams Mix* [1952], *4'33"* [1952], *HPSCHD* [1969], *Roaratorio* [1979], and *Europeras 1 & 2* [1987].) Additionally, silent compositions of the past, like Allais's, were meant to be silent, in the sense of being without or having the absence of sound. Cage's work is not silent in this sense. It embraces the ordinary world of nonintentional sound; it is full of sounds and thereby challenges our past and traditional understandings and definitions of music.

This shift of conceptual understanding brought by Cage to music and listening is not unlike that Wittgenstein brings to philosophy and self-reflection. Certainly language and its grammar were talked about and taken seriously before *Philosophical Investigations* (posthumous, 1953). But ordinary language was considered primarily an instrument or a medium, of whatever importance, in helping us understand something else, in getting us from one place to another—not the fact in terms of which all is or comes to be. And silence is not for Cage but a resting point between sounds, a transition from one place to another. The harmony of sound and silence (like word and world) is nowhere better expressed than in *4'33"*. The philosopher in us all, *our* philosophy, benefits from and finds good in listening to Cage in general and to *4'33"* specifically.

E. *I–VI*

(Remarks on 98)

An illustration of the mesostics, the main body content, of *I–VI* is excerpted from the next-to-last and last page of lecture one. The spine words are "inconsistency" and "performance." The lectures were written to be read aloud. A space followed by an apostrophe indicates a new breath. Syllables that would not normally be accented but should be are printed in bold type.

Is **a** '

aNd under

from whiCh

the tOp

aNd warfare

behavior followS

dogma natIion

of aS

planeT

arE ' elevated

iN washington

whiCh ' behavior

is ' alwaYs

•

image of something ' in this case ' we're comParing '

nichi nichi korE ko nichi '

fRom

oF

is accOmplished

constantly Replenished

Much

exAmple of

No

musiCians to plan

short of saying what constitutional rEforms are to be introduced

Parts for which

thE mind

that confRonts us

inFluences the means '

let sOunds be

stRaight

Music is

of thinking Are '

with oNe eye one does not

Cannot

thE '

Parts for which

thE mind

that confRonts us

oF

is accOmplished

stRaight '

Music is

of thinking Are '

with oNe eye one does not

Cannot

short of saying what constitutional rEforms are to be introduced

•

Chapter Seven
Index of Names

(Remarks on First and Second Books)

Numbers refer to the numbered "remarks" of the text, chapter references (c) are from the supplements section, and foreword (f) and preliminary remarks (pr) refer, respectively, to the foreword of the book and to the two prior paragraphs to each of the first two books.

Acknowledgments

*T*he writing of this book began in 2002 and had no readers other than myself for several years. In 2005 my thinking reached a point of momentary stability and I ask my friend Sarah Beckwith to look at the book and answer one question: Was it at all intelligible? She responded positively and encouraged me to let others see it. I then asked two other friends Toril Moi and David Paletz to respond to the same question. Beyond my expectations they encouraged me to seek formal publication of the book. This was something I had thought little about since it was a book for a few friends and I was pleased enough with that. After receiving a similar suggestion from other readers, who now had the circulating text, I considered its possible publication but did not quite know where to turn. Again, Toril, David, and Sarah were invaluable and helped me find a proper place, which became quite fortunately Paradigm Publishers. I thank each of them most deeply for their intellectual support and continuing friendship.

The principal reviewers of the text for Paradigm Publishers, Ralph Berry, Tim Gould, and Stanley Cavell were essential to the progress of the work and I am grateful to them for their attention and kindness. Additionally, Stanley, like so many times before, gave me many words of wisdom about ordinary language philosophy. His thinking and writing over the last half century have cast a great and wonderful light over all that I do.

Bill Duckworth and Mike Payne, friends of long standing, read drafts of the text and talked with me on several occasions about my arguments. They each gave me important encouragement and advice that I took very much to heart. My daughter, Leonore, listened constantly to me on various subjects of the text and she greatly sharpened my thinking about biology and ethics with her questions. Lester Miller, Leonore's husband, also talked with me about the text several times and was very helpful during a discussion on ethics and Schopenhauer. Liz Lewis, a close friend of many years, added to that conversation on Schopenhauer and she has asked numerous good questions about Dostoevsky over the years. Tony De Ritis has engaged me in discussions about music and interdisciplinary study for well over a decade and he has helped clarify my thinking on the topics of this text in innumerable ways. I thank them all for their patience, and for being so giving of their time to a project that could not have seemed clear given what I was saying to them.

My wife, Ona, is the love and strength of my life. Each day she listens to me and helps guide my thinking and feelings. Whatever my frustrations she lovingly provides me with proper perspectives of concern and importance. I could not have written this book, or done much else, without her.

Jennifer Knerr and Jessica Priest, have been inspired editors. They have helped beyond the normal expectations. Bringing a text of this type into a manageable form is a task they have performed admirably and I thank them both for their great diligence and careful attention. Additionally, I thank the managing editor Carol Smith and copy editor Jon Howard. They made my work, even with its many twists and turns, quite presentable. How they each, and the Paradigm Publishers in general, tolerated me and this text is not easy to understand. I am quite appreciative.

About the Author

Richard Fleming is the author of numerous books in ordinary language philosophy and contemporary music, including *First Word Philosophy* (2004) and *The State of Philosophy* (1993). He edited *Sound and Light* (1996) and *John Cage at Seventy-Five* (1989) with the contemporary musician William Duckworth. He regularly teaches philosophy and general humanities. His recent seminars include *"Reading the Philosophical Investigations*—Remark by Remark," Duke University, 2008–2009 and "Cage: Experimentation, Chance, Silence, Anarchism," Fusion Art Exchange, New York, 2007–2009.

MEDIA and POWER

David L. Paletz,
Series Editor, Duke University